P9-CDI-678

"This book will be invaluable to families choosing or considering a homeschooling option for their child with ASD. In an easily accessible question-and-answer format, the authors provide practical advice and a wealth of resources that will get parents started, support them through common challenges, and help them create a curriculum that meets not only the academic but also the social and behavioral needs of their child. This book provides a beacon of hope to families struggling with educational options for their child."

—*Sally Ozonoff, Ph.D.,* endowed professor, University of California–Davis, M.I.N.D. Institute

"This is an excellent sourcebook helping parents make informed decisions about homeschooling their children with ASD. Parents will learn how to schedule lessons across the day to incorporate social and academic learning in an environment that balances sensory and mental health needs. All parents, even those not considering homeschooling, will find this book helpful, as it encourages us to foster active learning in the home environment."

—*Michelle Garcia Winner,* founder of the Social Thinking treatment approach and speech language pathologist, San Jose, CA

"A *must* read for parents and teachers who need guidance and encouragement while teaching children with ASD!"

—*Cathy Stenzel,* mother of son with autism

"I appreciated reading well-researched information on the home school experience that actually follows the rules."

—*Diane Youtsey,* director of special education, Eureka (CA) Union School District

"This book is a 'life-line' to parents who homeschool children with autism. The authors have wonderful insight, recommendations, and thoughtful ideas for these parents."

—*Debbie Baehler,* autism specialist, Lassen County (CA) Office of Education

JOSSEY-BASS TEACHER

Jossey-Bass Teacher provides educators and parents with practical knowledge and tools to create a positive and lifelong impact on student learning. We offer classroom-tested and research-based teaching resources for a variety of grade levels and subject areas. Whether you are a parent, teacher, or another professional working with children in grades K-12, we want to help you make every learning experience successful.

From ready-to-use learning activities to the latest teaching framework, our value-packed books provide insightful, practical, and comprehensive materials on the topics that matter most. We hope to become your trusted source for the best ideas from the most experienced and respected experts in the field.

HOMESCHOOLING THE CHILD WITH AUTISM

Answers to the Top Questions
Parents and Professionals Ask

PATRICIA SCHETTER AND
KANDIS LIGHTHALL

Foreword
By Jeanette McAfee, M.D.

JOSSEY-BASS
A Wiley Imprint
www.josseybass.com

Copyright © 2009 by John Wiley & Sons, Inc. All rights reserved.

Published by Jossey-Bass
A Wiley Imprint
989 Market Street, San Francisco, CA 94103-1741—www.josseybass.com

No part of this publication may be reproduced, stored in a retrieval system, or transmitted in any form or by any means, electronic, mechanical, photocopying, recording, scanning, or otherwise, except as permitted under Section 107 or 108 of the 1976 United States Copyright Act, without either the prior written permission of the publisher, or authorization through payment of the appropriate per-copy fee to the Copyright Clearance Center, Inc., 222 Rosewood Drive, Danvers, MA 01923, 978-750-8400, fax 978-646-8600, or on the Web at www.copyright.com. Requests to the publisher for permission should be addressed to the Permissions Department, John Wiley & Sons, Inc., 111 River Street, Hoboken, NJ 07030, 201-748-6011, fax 201-748-6008, or online at www.wiley.com/go/permissions.

Readers should be aware that Internet Web sites offered as citations and/or sources for further information may have changed or disappeared between the time this was written and when it is read.

Limit of Liability/Disclaimer of Warranty: While the publisher and author have used their best efforts in preparing this book, they make no representations or warranties with respect to the accuracy or completeness of the contents of this book and specifically disclaim any implied warranties of merchantability or fitness for a particular purpose. No warranty may be created or extended by sales representatives or written sales materials. The advice and strategies contained herein may not be suitable for your situation. You should consult with a professional where appropriate. Neither the publisher nor author shall be liable for any loss of profit or any other commercial damages, including but not limited to special, incidental, consequential, or other damages.

Jossey-Bass books and products are available through most bookstores. To contact Jossey-Bass directly call our Customer Care Department within the U.S. at 800-956-7739, outside the U.S. at 317-572-3986, or fax 317-572-4002.

Jossey-Bass also publishes its books in a variety of electronic formats. Some content that appears in print may not be available in electronic books.

Library of Congress Cataloging-in-Publication Data

Schetter, Patricia, date
 Homeschooling the child with autism: answers to the top questions parents and professionals ask / Patricia Schetter and Kandis Lighthall.—1st ed.
  p. cm.
 Includes bibliographical references and index.
 ISBN 978-0-470-29256-3 (pbk.)
  1. Autistic children—Education. 2. Home schooling. I. Lighthall, Kandis, 1948-
II. Title.
 LC4717.S33 2009
 371.94—dc22

                                                    2008041497

Printed in the United States of America
FIRST EDITION
PB Printing   10 9 8 7 6 5 4 3 2 1

THE AUTHORS

Patricia Schetter and **Kandis Lighthall** both have master's degrees and have over fifty-five years of combined experience working with students who have special needs. Since 1999, they have worked collaboratively serving students with Autism Spectrum Disorders (ASD), their families, and educators. Their philosophy is to develop practical strategies that are based on current research, while being easy to implement. Their goal is to provide professional development to those who work with and care for individuals with ASD so that they may improve the quality of education and life for individuals with this disability.

Their collaboration has produced many seminars for educators, paraprofessionals, parents, and administrators. They have given presentations at state and national conferences, school districts, and agencies. In 2005, they developed an academic course series for the University of California at Davis that comprehensively covers ASD. Students completing the series receive a Special Studies Award in Autism.

Both authors have published multiple works. Schetter has authored *Learning the R.O.P.E.S. for Improved Executive Functioning* (2004), "Executive Dysfunction in Autism Spectrum Disorder from Research to Practice," in L. Metzler (ed.), *Executive*

Function in Education (2007), and *Autism Program Development and Review Protocols: APDAR* (2007). Lighthall has published *The School Participation Checklist: A Tool for Measuring Student Classroom Behavior* (2005), *What Makes School Great? Friends! Activities to Build Autism Awareness and Develop Friendships* (2006), *I Have a Friend with Autism: Activity Booklet* (2006), and *R.E.A.D.Y. for Inclusion: A Step by Step Process for Assessing and Implementing Successful Inclusive Education for Students with Autism Spectrum Disorders* (2007). In 2008, they coauthored *White Boards Words and Thoughts.*

The real reason they continue their work in this field is seen clearly in this photograph. It is the smile of success and friendship that they receive when they work with students such as Ethan, who is pictured with them in his "Hug Picture." Student, family, and educator success is the big reward that continually motivates them to do a better job. Their mission is to help others become the best that they can be.

Authors Kandis Lighthall and Patricia Schetter

CONTENTS

6 Questions for Homeschooling Parents 199

7 Questions for Homeschooled Children on the Autism Spectrum 213

Glossary of Terms and Acronyms 223
Notes 243
Index 253

ACKNOWLEDGMENTS

We want to acknowledge the contributions of the mothers who took time from their very busy schedules to complete our questionnaire and discuss issues they have experienced while homeschooling their own children. Their comments added great depth to this book. We would like the readers to know that these wonderful women are more than mothers who lovingly care for their families. We would also like to honor them for all the qualities that make them so special and thank them for their efforts, which will provide others with the insight needed to either begin or sustain homeschooling their child. You are all greatly appreciated for everything you do.

We would also like to acknowledge and extend our sincere thanks to the parents and professionals who took the time to read our completed manuscript and provide valuable feedback. Your support and commitment to this project and the lives of children on the autism spectrum continues to make a difference for many.

We would like to dedicate this book to families.

First, we dedicate this book to the families of children with Autism Spectrum Disorders who have shared so much with us during our careers.

Second, we dedicate this book to our families who have supported us in our efforts to develop publications that will make a difference in the lives of many.

FOREWORD

As Patricia Schetter and Kandis Lighthall point out in this well-organized, practical, and encouraging guide to homeschooling children with autism, a homeschool environment can be the single most effective place for some children with autism to learn, grow, and achieve their maximum potential. In many cases, a child learning at home will acquire far more knowledge and experience in social skills, academic skills, life skills, and executive functioning than he or she would absorb in a typical classroom setting.

Homeschooling the Child with Autism is organized in an easy-to-read question-and-answer format. It is packed full of specific, how-to information that is supplemented by numerous comments and tips from seasoned homeschooling teachers. At the end of the book, there is an invaluable collection of interviews with home-schooled students who have Autism Spectrum Disorders (ASDs). This section gives the reader the pros and cons (mostly pros) of homeschooling from the students' perspectives and will be helpful to anyone who is thinking of homeschooling.

Because one of the biggest challenges for kids with autism is developing social skills, it is fair to ask how a homeschooled child with an ASD can be given sufficient exposure to social situations. After all, the average classroom has anywhere from fifteen to forty students who could socialize with the child, whereas the typical homeschool environment may provide only one parent—or a parent plus siblings—to interact with the child. Nevertheless, a homeschool environment may actually provide the child with far superior quality and frequency of social interactions, because it gives parents control over the child's social environment. Unlike the typical teacher, who is responsible for multiple students in a limited physical environment (that is, the school campus), a parent-teacher can choose the people with whom the child will interact as well as the places and situations where the interaction occurs. The parent-teacher can set up playdates, study sessions, and community outings in a wide assortment of places with a variety of people who are sympathetic to the child with autism.

While students in typical school settings have opportunities to go on field trips, usually this is limited to one or two trips per semester. In contrast, the home-school teacher can incorporate community trips into the curriculum on a daily basis and has an almost unlimited number of places to teach social skills lessons, ranging from playdates with peers at home to community trips to shops, theaters, and restaurants.

In addition, the homeschool teacher can teach discrete social skills initially by using a formal lesson format and later by encouraging the student to use these skills during the rest of the day. This technique of teaching social skills in small steps and then prompting the use of these skills in everyday life maximizes a student's generalization of the skills. It is much easier for a homeschool teacher to accomplish this—and in a way that is tailored specifically to the individual child—than it is for a classroom teacher who must keep track of the needs of multiple students each day.

The homeschooling parent is, in effect, a designer of the social environment in which the child will learn to trust or not trust and to accept or shun relationships with other people. It is a well-known fact that individuals with Autism Spectrum Disorders are more at risk for suffering cruel, unremitting bullying and teasing at school and elsewhere. The homeschool teacher can screen out potentially negative social contacts and can provide specific training to the people with whom the child has the most frequent contact. The inability of the autistic child to "read" other people's thoughts and intentions can make the social world a confusing—and sometimes frightening—place. Severe problems with understanding unwritten social rules and distinguishing friend from foe can be so overwhelming to these children that they end up simply withdrawing into their own inner world, a world which they tend to fill with predictable objects and rules rather than with people and the unpredictability invariably associated with them. A homeschool environment allows children with ASDs to participate in social relationships in a controlled and positive way so that they do not experience the need to withdraw from others.

Authors Schetter and Lighthall have done an excellent job of debunking the myth that only credentialed teachers can teach academic subjects successfully. In the ideal educational setting, each child is taught using the methods that best fit that child's strengths, weaknesses, and learning style. Unfortunately, in the average classroom teachers often are forced to teach according to the skills and needs of the average student, a situation that all too often doesn't reach those students who are either high performers or low performers in a given subject area. Children with ASDs are noted for their complex and unique qualities, and rarely do they fit into the category of "average." Much more commonly they present an uneven profile of academic abilities, often excelling in one academic area while performing at a level significantly below average in other areas. A homeschool teacher can adjust for these differences much more easily, with the end result being a truly "individualized" curriculum for the autistic student. In addition, as the authors point out, large-scale studies have demonstrated that homeschooled students have "achievement test scores (that are) exceptionally high" and that "the students who had received the longest duration of homeschooling appeared to have the greatest achievement advantage."

Lastly, a parent considering homeschooling his or her child should not feel isolated in this endeavor. In Part Three, Schetter and Lighthall provide a comprehensive and highly useful list of resources to aid parents in getting help with the homeschooling process.

One of the more obvious benefits of homeschooling is the ability to teach life skills throughout the school day. Learning how to prepare meals and take care of a house are skills that are arguably just as important as academic achievement when viewed from a long-term perspective. A further advantage of homeschooling is that math, reading, science, and other subjects can be incorporated into life skills lessons.

Executive functioning deficits in children with ASDs can wreak havoc in their ability to self-monitor and to plan, organize, and complete tasks. Schetter and Lighthall's book includes an excellent summary of abilities that can be compromised by poor executive functioning as well as tips on how to improve executive functioning in children with ASDs.

This book is a must-read for anyone who is considering homeschooling their child with autism. It shows clearly and concisely the benefits, while considering the potential drawbacks, of homeschooling, and it answers the most frequently asked questions regarding how to go about doing it.

In conclusion, perhaps the greatest value of this book lies in its message that homeschooling can be the best alternative for a particular child, and that yes, you can do it—and not only do it well, but do it exceptionally well. In fact, the homeschooling experience can be not only successful but highly rewarding for both parent and child.

Yuba City, California —Jeanette McAfee, M.D., homeschooling
October 2008 mother, author, and founder/director of
Social Solutions, a clinic for individuals
with high functioning autism
and Asperger's Syndrome

Introduction

Autism is the fastest growing developmental disability in the United States, with current estimates indicating that it affects 1 in every 150 children.[1] The first World Autism Awareness Day, held on April 2, 2008, reflects the global impact of this disability. Autism impacts a child's ability to think and learn in a typical way. A host of challenges present themselves in a traditional school program, including sensory, social, and communication challenges, along with struggles accessing the necessary academic accommodations. Increasing numbers of families are opting to minimize this stress on their children with ASD by homeschooling. Families indicate that homeschooling decreases the external stressors the child is exposed to in traditional school settings, and it relieves much of the anxiety that often results from poor academic performance or behavioral challenges. Homeschooling allows parents to directly address the core deficits of communication, social skills, social understanding, and organizational thinking, while providing functional academics that are real-world and experientially based. Instruction can truly be individualized to encompass the student's interests and learning style. Instruction can be based on personal experiences and motivation. Because parents have the highest vested interest in their child, they are able to maintain the motivation to work through challenges and find what works for that particular child.

Along with the advantages of homeschooling come several challenges, including accessing professional support, providing training and materials, and setting up opportunities for social learning and peer involvement. Additionally, the parent or teachers must possess a great deal of skill and creativity related to curriculum design and behavioral management.

This book is written for parents who have chosen to homeschool their children with ASD, as well as for those who are considering this option. Additionally, we hope that the extended family, professional educators, school administrators, and private providers will use this book as a resource for better understanding ASD and to increase their understanding of homeschooling as a viable and cost-effective option for providing an appropriate educational experience to children with this disability.

This book answers twenty of the most commonly asked questions related to homeschooling a child with ASD in an easy-to-use question-and-answer format. We provide factual information along with practical ideas and strategies for addressing common challenges. Valuable resources and case examples are provided throughout. In addition, contributions from several parents who have chosen to homeschool provide the reader with real-life insight. Most valuable, however, are the perspectives of their children. Through their stories, the reader develops a true appreciation of the importance of providing homeschooling as part of a continuum of educational options. The book can be read cover to cover for a comprehensive picture of homeschooling a child with ASD, or it can be used as a resource to answer specific questions or challenges.

1

Questions About Autism Spectrum Disorders (ASD)

1 What Is ASD and How Do the Core Areas of Impairment Affect Students in a Traditional School Setting?

Autism Spectrum Disorder

Autism Spectrum Disorder (ASD) is a neurobiological impairment that impacts a child's development. The disability can be present from birth, with some of the symptoms being recognized by twelve months of age. These earliest symptoms include limited eye contact or failure to look at the eyes and faces of others, limited response to their name and to the social gestures of others, and impaired imitation of both sound and actions.[1] Other children with ASD appear to have a typical pattern of early development with a fairly sudden onset of symptoms and a loss of skills, including loss of words, eye contact, and play skills. This regressive subtype often becomes symptomatic between eighteen to twenty-four months of age.

The average age of diagnosis for Autistic Disorder is three years of age, but often individuals with fewer autistic symptoms, such as those with Pervasive Developmental Disorder–Not Otherwise Specified (PDD-NOS), or those with Asperger's Syndrome (AS), considered the highest functioning on the Autism Spectrum, are diagnosed much later. The average age of diagnosis for Asperger's Syndrome is eight to twelve years of age and is very often a second or third diagnostic label given to a child with the disability. Disorders such as Attention Deficit Disorder (ADD), Obsessive Compulsive Disorder (OCD), or other Behavioral Disorders, including Conduct Disorder (CD) and Oppositional Defiant Disorder (ODD), are often assigned first, typically by professionals who lack an understanding of ASD.

Autism is referred to as a "spectrum disorder" because of the wide variability of functioning seen in individuals with the disability. The core areas that are impaired in ASD are communication and socialization skills. An additional area that is affected is restrictive and repetitive patterns of behavior. People with ASD may engage in self-stimulating behaviors such as spinning or rocking or repetitious routines such as lining things up or insisting that things be done in a very specific order. Children with Asperger's Syndrome (AS) are often highly verbal, but tend to use unusual language and may perseverate on one specific topic or have an intense area of interest. Children with classic Autistic Disorder have a delay in the development of spoken language and often use *echolalic* or repetitive speech or they may remain nonverbal, having no way to communicate basic needs and desires except through their behavior.

It is generally accepted that children with ASD face varying levels of challenges processing sensory information.[2] The literature reports that people with ASD process sensory experiences differently from people who do not have ASD.[3] It is estimated that around two-thirds of children with ASD also have significant sensory processing issues that impact their ability to function in one or more life-skill domains. Many with ASD experience a high sensitivity to touch, sound, light, or movement that results in behavioral refusal and avoidance of a variety of situations and activities. Most children develop a set of protective responses, including covering their ears, actively moving away from or avoiding people, or avoiding highly stimulating settings. Some develop coping skills to get through "overstimulating" activities, but may eventually act out or become exhausted by their efforts. This exhaustion looks like complete shutdown, where the individual will not respond even to activities they know how to perform.

Impacts in Traditional School Settings

Traditional school settings are usually highly active and interactive environments. People with ASD face many challenges tolerating and coping with the sensory stimulation. They are also challenged with recognizing, interpreting, and responding to social situations; understanding all the facets of the academic task demands; and processing a great deal of verbal communication. For students with ASD, traditional school settings may feel like being in rush-hour traffic in a strange city, on a rainy day with the dog barking in the backseat. While this is possible, it is also exhausting!

People with ASD have high verbal skills and average to above-average intelligence as measured on standardized IQ tests. They tend to have relative strengths in many academic areas, including decoding (many are hyperlexic or self-taught readers), math calculation (some becoming brilliant mathematicians, engineers, or physicists), and other academic areas that require memorization or implementation of rules and procedures. These same individuals have extreme impairments in using and understanding nonverbal communication, in recognizing and responding to their emotions or the emotions of others, and in taking other people's perspectives and responding in socially appropriate ways. They may also be highly rigid in their thinking and behavior and respond inappropriately to a change in routine or a new expectation.

Although individuals with ASD may have excellent vocabulary skills, they also tend to interpret language literally. This often results in problems interpreting what other people mean in their everyday speech. For example, the teacher might say, "Everyone take your seat." The student with ASD might respond with "Take it where?" This is not noncompliance or sarcasm. The student with ASD interprets the instruction in the literal sense and may make a mistake in his attempt to follow the teacher's direction. Teachers who do not understand the nature of this disability might misinterpret the student's behavior and assume that the student is being willful, oppositional, or comical. The more frequently these "miscommunications" occur, the more anxious the student may become. He may spend a great deal of time during the school day attempting to interpret the teacher's instructions or the comments and slang words or phrases used by peers.

Academic areas that require mental flexibility, problem solving, prediction, and perspective taking are a struggle for individuals with ASD. Many do very well in school until the curriculum shifts at around third grade. Up until that point, the focus of learning is on facts and procedures, which are a relative strength for these learners. At around third grade, students are expected to engage in more complex learning, which includes making predictions, making inferences, and solving complex problems. Once this shift occurs, many students with ASD begin to fall behind or become increasingly frustrated with school and homework.

Challenges in Middle School and High School

Another shift that is very challenging for those with ASD occurs in the late elementary grades and middle school. Teachers begin to expect students to maintain the organization of their own work space, materials, and assignments.

In the early grades, teachers provide a high level of organizational structure and support. This is accomplished through classroom design, such as having learning centers where materials are all prepared in advance and ready for students to use when they arrive at the center. Teachers also provide a highly predictable and structured schedule that includes regular routines each day, homework packets that are broken up over the week, regular standing tests, and activity times. The teachers will lead their students through complex assignments like book reports by breaking them into manageable chunks, providing explicit step-by-step procedures, and listing student expectations. These strategies provide students with ASD the physical, temporal, and cerebral organizational structure that they need to succeed. Given that students with ASD lack the hardwired organizational skills, also called *executive functioning capabilities,* to manage their own physical and cerebral organization, the highly structured environment, predictable schedule, and orderly presentation of assignments are critical for students with ASD.

In contrast, when students reach the later elementary grades and middle-school years, the teacher's expectation is that the student has the ability to manage his own physical space and assignments. The teacher assumes that the student has developed the skills to organize his desk, locker, backpack, and his own assignments such as homework, reading, research, reports, and test preparation without additional teacher direction. Teachers also expect the student to manage his own time by using downtime for studying, organizing himself, and preparing for upcoming events or assignments. School can quickly become overwhelming for a student with ASD or for any student who does not have highly developed organizational skills or the executive functioning capabilities to manage these organizational processes. Executive functioning will be discussed in greater detail in Chapter Four, Question 13.

Impacts of Fine and Gross Motor Challenges

Many students with ASD struggle with motor coordination, including the gross motor skills that are required for sports and P.E., as well as the fine motor skills that are required for handwriting. The expectation that students in traditional education programs will participate in group sports puts social and performance pressures on those with ASD who struggle with social skills and motor coordination. Physical education classes and recess can be very stressful times for students with ASD. These are also time periods where students with ASD can be victimized or teased relentlessly for their lack of physical prowess or for their quirky behaviors.

The fine motor demands of writing that are expected in traditional schools and the rigid nature of the schedule, where a great deal of written output is expected within a short period of time, are also a high source of stress and oftentimes failure. When provided with an alternative form of output, such as keyboarding or dictation, students with ASD can perform quite well. These accommodations may be challenging to access or implement in a traditional school setting. Even if they are available, many with ASD do not want the stigma of using the necessary accommodations in the traditional school settings because these accommodations set them apart from their peers and make them feel "different."

Emotional Impacts

Adolescents with ASD are at high risk for depression and anxiety. Many of these students are bright enough to recognize they are different, and it becomes hard to focus on their strengths when all they may see in a traditional school setting are their social, academic, or physical weaknesses. While on the surface, individuals with ASD may simply appear quirky, they are fully affected by the core deficits of Autism and the effects on learning and behavior. Because of high verbal skills and academic strengths in certain areas, teachers often have unrealistic academic and social expectations for some ASD students. The student may be able to do certain aspects of an assignment, but may struggle with others. He may be able to explain how to do something, but cannot execute the plan without ongoing prompting and support. He may want to have friends and work in a group, but lack the social skills and understanding to do this successfully. These types of academic and social frustrations often result in acting out or shutting down in traditional school programs.

Students with Cognitive Delays and Severe Autism

It is estimated that 75 percent of individuals with Autistic Disorder also have some degree of cognitive impairment.[4] While there are no outward physical symptoms of ASD, individuals who function at the middle or lower end of the spectrum are often easier to recognize than those with high-functioning forms of ASD. Their unusual speech (echolalia) or inability to use words to communicate and higher levels of repetitive motor behaviors (self-stimulating behaviors) make the disability more visible and recognizable to others. Teachers and peers may be more tolerant of behaviors or have more realistic academic and social expectations of a child with moderate forms of ASD in traditional educational settings. An issue faced by these students is the tendency of teachers and aides to overprompt or provide such high levels of support that the student never learns how to do things independently.

Time spent in a general education classroom may be overstimulating to a student with more severe ASD, which may result in higher rates of sensory regulating or self-stimulatory behaviors and missed instructional opportunities. It is also very challenging to address the functional, behavioral, and communication needs of a more-involved student in a traditional inclusive classroom setting. As a result, students with more severe ASD may be educated in special day classrooms (SDC). While this more controlled setting may facilitate academic, functional skills, and communication growth and promote better behavioral regulation, it may also result in missed opportunities for social development. Even when these students are in proximity to typically developing peers, such as during recess, social teaching opportunities are difficult to capture in traditional school programs.

Recess on a traditional school campus is a noisy and active time. The vast space of the traditional playground and the lack of structure make it challenging to be able to teach or facilitate social interactions. Students with ASD may also have great difficulty in generalizing the skills learned at school to other settings such as home and the community.

Problematic Behaviors

Sensory differences, social avoidance, and lack of appropriate play or leisure skills often result in unconventional behavioral patterns. Severe behavior may make teachers fearful of working with a student, and may lead peers to steer away from interactions. Individuals with ASD require higher levels of support, more specialized teaching strategies, and frequent reinforcement for engaging in appropriate behavior. When unable to communicate or understand the expectations of others, problematic behaviors such as aggression, throwing tantrums, bolting, or screaming may develop. Individually designed positive behavior support plans (BSP) that include teaching prosocial and adaptive responses are essential for success. These highly individualized teaching plans must be implemented consistently in order to be most effective. This can be challenging in traditional educational settings, as the student may encounter many teachers or specialists throughout the day, each with his or her own unique way of working with the student. Consistent implementation of teaching and behavior support plans requires a great deal of communication and planning time amongst team members, which is often difficult to achieve in traditional school programs.

Physical Signs of Stress

A study by Richdale and Prior (1992) found that people with ASD have a tendency toward cortisol hypersecretion (a hormone associated with stress) during their school hours.[5] In their study, these researchers found that the same subjects had relatively normal levels of cortisol secretion during nonschool hours. This provides evidence that traditional school settings elicit a stress response in people with ASD. These findings are further clarified by Corbett and her colleagues (2006), who found that people with ASD had increased cortisol reactions compared to neurotypical controls when presented with any novel or threatening event.[6] Due to the level of stimulation and the unpredictable nature of a typical school environment, we can ascertain that the nature of traditional school settings is very stressful to children with ASD. This stress impacts them physically as well as behaviorally as they attempt to cope.

Necessity to Provide a Continuum of Options for Students with ASD

While it is not impossible for a student with ASD to access a high-quality and appropriate educational program in a traditional school setting, this scenario does present many challenges. The needs and challenges of the individual child, as well as the structure, training, and readiness of the school staff, must all be considered. With all the right supports and training in place, many with

ASD can thrive in traditional public education. However, it must also be recognized that the traditional school setting may not meet the needs of all students and families.

The National Research Council (2001) recommends that a continuum of placement options be available to students with ASD.[7] This continuum can range from full-time placement in a general education classroom to a special day classroom, to home- and community-based instruction. By having a continuum of options available, public school programs will be more likely to succeed with this challenging population of learners. In addition, they may be better able to collaborate with families who believe in and desire homeschooling for their child.

2   Is There Peer-Reviewed Research That Supports Homeschooling for Students with ASD?

At the present time, a comprehensive research literature review on the topic of *homeschooling students on the Autism Spectrum* yielded no formal results; however, numerous studies indicate the importance of parental involvement in the educational and treatment programs of children with ASD. A 1998 study conducted by Sally Rogers reports that all efficacious treatments of young children with ASD involve the parents in some role.[8] Ivar Lovaas and colleagues found that children whose treatment took place in the home setting, where parents were actively involved, made significant gains on measures of IQ and expressive and receptive language. These home-educated students appeared to have a greater treatment advantage compared with those who received traditional special education services through the public school.[9]

Further studies have indicated that parents can be highly effective as teachers of their children with special needs[10] and can demonstrate equal levels of success in running an intervention program as trained professionals.[11] Additionally, several studies have shown that with parent training in the implementation of effective educational strategies, the level of family stress and the depressive symptoms often seen in mothers of children with ASD can be reduced significantly.[12] Happier and more frequent parent-child interactions and more positive parent-child communications have also been shown as a result of parent training in effective educational interventions.[13] Studies have also demonstrated that as parents are better able to manage behaviors and as more adaptive skills are acquired, families benefit by their ability to access community and leisure activities.[14]

Although there have been no empirically validated studies indicating the treatment effects of homeschooling children with ASD specifically, it is clear from the previously mentioned studies that parents are a vital component of effective educational treatment and that both the parent and child can benefit from parent-implemented educational strategies.

General Homeschooling Research

As we look to the research literature to guide us, it is important to reference the general research on homeschooling and the research that has been conducted in other special needs populations. This research can help to answer some of the questions, criticisms, or possible misinterpretations about homeschooling that many cite in opposition to this educational choice.

Homeschooling and Academic Success

Many people fear that children who receive homeschool instruction are missing out on the valuable learning opportunities that promote success and that their academic achievement will be compromised as a result. Quite the opposite has been documented.

In 1998, the largest survey and testing program for students in homeschools to date was conducted by Dr. Lawrence Rudner, involving 20,760 kindergarten through twelfth-grade homeschooled students. Participants were administered either the Iowa Tests of Basic Skills (ITBS) or the Tests of Achievement and Proficiency (TAP), depending on their current grade level. The parents also responded to a questionnaire regarding background and demographic information. The findings of this study indicate that the achievement test scores of this group of homeschooled students was exceptionally high, with the median scores falling in the 70th to 80th percentile. Additionally, 25 percent of homeschooled students from the survey were enrolled in one or more grade levels above their age-matched traditionally schooled peers. The students who had been homeschooled the longest appeared to have the greatest achievement advantage. Although this was not a scientifically controlled study, the results do demonstrate that homeschoolers can accomplish excellent results in academic domains.[15]

Further support for homeschooling to yield academic results is supplied by the 1997 study of 5,402 homeschooled students entitled, "Strengths of Their Own: Home Schoolers Across America." This study demonstrated that homeschoolers, on the average, outperformed their counterparts in the public schools by 30 to 37 percentile points in all subjects. This study also indicated that the longer the child had been receiving homeschooling, the greater the advantage.[16]

Speculations about why the advantages are so great include the individualized attention and instruction that is provided in homeschooling. Additionally, the student can be assessed for skill mastery on a more frequent basis, moving at their own pace through the curriculum, and problems can be addressed and corrected more quickly. The efficiency of instruction is also increased in homeschooling, with less downtime and more opportunities for learning and instruction. All of these advantages apply whether the learner is a neurotypical child, a gifted child, or a child with ASD. Given these implications of the research findings, one could assume that the same or similar results would occur with specialized populations. These have all been identified as advantages seen in homeschooling a child with ASD.

Homeschooling and Social Skills

One of the biggest criticisms and misinterpretations about homeschooling is that the student will miss out on social learning opportunities and, as a result, his social skills will suffer. This is probably the most common criticism and reaction about homeschooling a child with ASD. Several researchers have found an overwhelmingly positive picture for homeschooled students' socialization. Not only are homeschoolers provided with opportunities that foster positive social interactions, they also receive protection from many sources of negative socialization.

Research has shown us that home-educated children are in fact exposed to nearly the same number of social contacts as traditionally educated children. The important factor, however, is not the number of contacts, but appears to be the quality of social interactions. According to April Chatham-Carpenter, homeschoolers are exposed to more positive social interactions that promote prosocial behavior rather than negative social interactions that may promote negative social behaviors and attitudes. Researcher Richard Medlin (2000) substantiated this finding with his study comparing 70 homeschooled students to 70 traditionally schooled students. His data indicate that self-concept was higher for the homeschooled students, who also presented with significantly fewer behavioral disorders.[17]

It is clear that there is a growing body of evidence indicating that social skills are not negatively, but in fact, positively impacted through homeschooling. Again, if this holds true with neurotypical children, one can assume that similar results might be found in children with ASD.

Homeschooling Research with Other Special Needs Populations

A growing body of evidence supports the effects of homeschooling specialized populations of learners. While the breadth of this research is meager now, we expect that as homeschooling continues to gain momentum, especially with special needs learners, the body of research will accelerate.

A study conducted by Duvall and colleagues (1997) found that special needs students who were homeschooled exceeded the gains in reading, spelling, and math of their peers who were educated in traditional, special education settings. An exploratory study by Duvall and colleagues in 2004 of students with ADD indicated that homeschooled students were academically engaged about two times as often as traditionally schooled students and experienced greater gains in reading and math. Because of the small sample sizes and lack of replication of these studies, no causal relation can be claimed; however, these preliminary finding are highly suggestive that homeschooling children with special learning needs can be highly effective, perhaps more effective than traditional special education programs and services.[18]

Jacque Ensign, in a paper presented at the American Educational Research Association (April 15, 1998) entitled *Defying the Stereotypes of Special Education: Homeschooled Students,* reported her findings from a seven-year longitudinal study of four students with learning disabilities. Of the four students she followed, one had successfully graduated from high school and the other three were expected to complete the requirements for a high school diploma. All four students were also expected to continue with postsecondary education. This 100 percent graduation rate and anticipated postsecondary education is impressive when compared with the statistical averages for learning disabled students who are traditionally schooled (38 percent dropout rate and only 28 percent college attendance). While her data is anecdotal, it still lends support to the notion that student-centered, individualized programs that are typical in homeschooling yield very positive results in students with specialized learning needs.

We are seeing an increase in the popularity of homeschooling, both with typically developing and special needs children, and particularly students with ASD. As the numbers increase, so too will the research on the practice. This will provide us with a clearer picture of the benefits and drawbacks of homeschooling in this population. Research in this area will hopefully help to identify whether there are advantages to homeschooling for specific age groups or for children who fall in a certain range on the autism spectrum. We hope that future research will also provide some clear procedures and protocols to make the educational program most effective. At this point in time, we must draw from what information we have thus far and trust in good judgment and the implementation of best practice by those who make the homeschooling choice.

3 | Why Do Some Families of Children with ASD Consider Homeschooling?

Before addressing why families of children with ASD choose to homeschool, it must be acknowledged that historically a child's education began in the home with his or her parents and extended family members as teachers. Compulsory attendance in public schools did not begin to become mandatory until the mid-1800s when states began to enact laws requiring children to attend school.

A return to teaching children at home emerged again in the 1960s and 1970s when some families became disappointed with public education. Since then, the number of parents choosing to homeschool their children has substantially increased. The most recent research completed in the United States was conducted during 2002–2003 by the National Center for Educational Statistics (NCES) and published in 2006. This survey reveals that there has been a substantial increase in the number of students being homeschooled in this five-year period. The data indicated that in 1999 approximately 850,000 children were being homeschooled compared to 1,096,000 in 2003. The 2003 data show that 2.2 percent of the student-age population is in a homeschool program.[19] To read the complete report online, contact the National Center for Educational Statistics at http://nces.ed.gov.

The families who completed the NCES survey revealed that they chose to homeschool their children for many of the same reasons that families who have children with ASD do. The three main reasons listed by families surveyed for this book included safety, religious or moral concerns, and dissatisfaction with academic instruction. Both groups of homeschooling families, regardless of the child's ability or disability, share a core set of beliefs: that they understand best the educational needs of their child; that they can provide more time to the child; and that they can pass on the morals and value systems that are most important to their family.

Safety

Because of the social cognitive deficits that are present in children with ASD, they have a greater potential for victimization or being "put up to" things by peers. Many find themselves in trouble with school administrators or sometimes the law due to the lack of social understanding. This is a commonly cited reason for selecting to homeschool a child with ASD.

Parent
Perspective

I worried for my child's safety and that he would be a target of teasing.

—Ann Coe

His safety was a major issue since he had not developed the ability to understand deception. We felt that he might get taken advantage of in a school with over two thousand students. Additionally, he would have gone to school where the teachers just see him a few hours out of the week, and they would not understand his social delays and, therefore, would not be aware of the potential for danger.

—Connie Ajay

A Natural Continuation from In-Home Early Intervention Services

Families with children who have received an early diagnosis of autistic disorder before the age of thirty-six months may already be participating in an intensive early intervention program that is being carried out in their home. For these families it may feel more appropriate to continue the educational program at home when their child reaches school age. If the child's homeschooling program is to be provided through a public education homeschooling option, then roles and responsibilities need to be determined through the Individualized Education Program (IEP) process. If the parents choose to independently homeschool their child through a private school option, then supports and services become the family's responsibility as will be discussed in Question 9.

Dissatisfaction with Academic Instruction

It is well documented that a significant shortage of fully credentialed special educators exists in the United States.[20] In 2007 the
U.S. Department of Education reported that more than 10 percent
of teachers in special education positions lack the proper certifica-
tions. The greatest gap and shortage in fully qualified teachers is in
the area of severe disabilities, which is the authorization required to
provide services to children with ASD in most states. Data further
indicate that one in every five special education teachers leaves special education each year, increasing the gap and leaving many inex-
perienced teachers to provide special education services and
support. Compounding this problem is the lack of special and general educators who have received specific training in Autism
Spectrum Disorders. This shortage and the rapidly growing numbers of individuals with ASD translates into a major gap in the
public education system's ability to provide enough trained and
prepared professionals to effectively educate and support students
with ASD. This shortage has had a significant impact on families
who have a child with ASD. In cases where there is a lack of knowl-
edgeable professionals, this may result in families quickly becoming dissatisfied with classroom instruction. A national shortage of
speech therapists and occupational therapists contributes to the
problem of related services. The school system's difficulty in filling
professional positions often results in a family's dissatisfaction with
the services and supports their child may require to be successful
in a traditional school setting.

There is little, if any, training provided to general education
teachers or site-level administrators in the credentialing process
related to Autism Spectrum Disorders. Training for classroom
aides and support staff is often an afterthought, and because of
tight budgets, these people often do not receive any specific

training in ASD, evidence-based instructional strategies, or positive behavioral supports. There is a growing concern about these shortages and the significant need for more training in ASD. These concerns are cited by the National Research Council (2001), the California Legislative Blue Ribbon Commission on Autism (2007), as well as other public policy studies conducted around the nation.[21] The current state of affairs gives rise to several parental concerns, as illustrated below.

Parent Perspective

In my personal experience in dealing with families of children with ASD, the main reason for contemplating homeschooling is often frustration with the school system. The systemic lack of support in implementing the accommodations or modifications and lack of understanding of how the disability impacts the student's learning are common.

—Connie Ajay

Experiences dealing with school personnel may produce an abundance of negative energy that is draining and counterproductive. Parents often decide they would rather spend their time and energy dealing directly with their children, rather than continuing to confront school personnel.

—Karen Crum

There is a sense of frustration with the public school mainstream curriculum and the staff's lack of knowledge or training in how to help these special needs children have a chance in life.

—Michelle King

This sense of dissatisfaction by parents may arise soon after placing their child in traditional public school. Parents may immediately realize that it is not a good fit for their child and remove him or begin looking for alternatives. Other parents may keep their child enrolled in traditional school for a longer period of time. From our research and interviews, it appears that a common decision point to move to homeschooling occurs at around second or third grade. At this time in a child's school career, the simple behavioral concerns that may have been voiced in kindergarten and first grade have increased to issues that must be systematically addressed and resolved. Other natural transition points that prompt the consideration of homeschooling are moving to middle school or high school. The size of the campus, safety concerns, changing classes, and having multiple teachers are all reasons for

Parent Perspective

We chose to homeschool because Ian was about to start high school. He only had two teachers in junior high and had some problems and lots of stress there. I didn't think that six high school teachers would accommodate his learning differences enough to help him be successful. I didn't think communication between Ian, the teachers, and I would occur often enough, or quickly enough. I didn't think that he would adapt to the large, busy high school campus, where only a few people actually knew him. I didn't think much learning would go on in this distracting environment. The special education and resource classes (except math) were not appropriate for my son because of their lower academic level.

—Ann Coe

concern at these points in time. For some families reaching these transition points may have been a long and arduous journey peppered with many issues that may have felt insurmountable. Each transition may feel like starting over.

Emotional Health of the Child and Family

Additional reasons that parents of children with ASD choose to homeschool include reducing stress and anxiety and building self-esteem.

Parent Perspective

Parents may consider homeschool because many kids with ASD become very anxious in a traditional school setting. The anxiety can lead to behavior problems and depression that can have long-term negative effects. The constant anxiety is detrimental to healthy living and learning. The anxiety of the child with ASD usually affects the entire family system in a negative way. Homeschool produces new challenges, but they are often preferable to the chronic stress that traditional school creates. Students with ASD who have average or above-average intelligence often feel incompetent in traditional systems because they learn differently or respond differently from other students. They compare themselves to others in an environment where their gifts may not be recognized or utilized enough to compensate for their differences. At home, without constant comparison to neurotypical peers, students with ASD can learn to appreciate and feel good about themselves.

—Karen Crum

Social Opportunities and Extracurricular Activities

An additional reason parents of children with ASD choose to home-school is the social opportunities and the richness in appropriate extracurricular participation that can be created.

Lack of Focus on Self-Help and Life Skills

For some families of students with ASD, the increased national and state focus on academic achievement and standardized testing has had a negative impact. Even the alternate standardized testing for students with moderate to severe disabilities reduces important instructional time for students who have ASD along with cognitive or other delays.

Parents of children with significant delays want their child to be successful, but acknowledge that success is not always measured academically. These parents want their child to learn the self-help and life skills that will be the foundation for as independent a life as possible. Learning self-help and life skills requires the same systematic and direct instruction that any academic skill requires. However, for

Parent Perspective

Some people have asked about the social component, but this is not a problem since my child is now getting social opportunities in groups and with kids who share the same hobbies and interests. Now the social opportunities are more meaningful and joyful for my child because they are related to his special interests.

—Connie Ajay

students with more significant delays, instruction requires more practice and experiences in relevant and meaningful environments where the child will actually use the skills. This type of instruction, which is sometimes called community-based instruction, requires a very low student-to-staff ratio, adequate supports, and resources, which may not be available in a traditional school setting to the degree necessary for some students. This may cause frustration and dissatisfaction for parents and prompt them to choose to home-school their child who needs self-help and life skills instruction.

Bottom-Line Reasons for Choosing Homeschooling

Most of the parents we interviewed admitted that homeschooling was not something that they had anticipated doing. It was a decision that was made over time and based on many factors, and ultimately on the gut-level instinct that it was the best decision for their child at that time.

Parent Perspective

Most parents of children with ASD never planned to homeschool and would not be considering it if things were going well for their child at school.

—Janelle Lewis

2

Questions About Homeschooling

4 | What Are the Different Types of Homeschooling?

When any parents, including parents of children with ASD, make the decision to homeschool their child, they must determine the type of program they will follow. There are an array of homeschooling options parents may choose from that include public and private school options as well as a blend or an eclectic approach.

Public Homeschool or Independent Study

As parents are making homeschooling more of a mainstream option, the public school system is responding by creating programs that support this option. The structure of the public school home-schooling program will vary from district to district. Some school districts call this type of program "Independent Study"; others may call it "Homeschool." Because it is part of the public education system,

27

Parent Perspective

Some public homeschool programs are quite flexible about how you teach your child and others are quite dictatorial. Different homeschool facilitators will have different styles and personalities, and you need to decide and ask for one that fits your style. If you have your own strong ideas about how to teach and do not want to follow the rules and assessment schedules of public schools, you can take on homeschooling completely independently as a private school provider (depending on your state laws). Of course, you can always ask for help from experienced homeschoolers when you have a question or problem.

—Karen Crum

this type of homeschool program is provided free and is required to abide by the laws and regulations that apply to any public school program. This means that the parents' and child's rights are the same as if the child was educated in a traditional public school program.

Typically, this type of program offers curriculum materials and regular support from a credentialed teacher. Some programs provide scheduled opportunities to come together with other students and families. Using a public school program may also allow a student on an Individual Education Plan (IEP) to access some of the designated instructional services (DIS) specified in the IEP, such as speech or occupational therapy. Entitlement to special education service will be discussed in greater detail in Question 9.

Public Charter Schools

These are relatively new models of public instruction that often offer a homeschooling component. The first charter school law was passed in 1991. The three principals of charter schools are choice, accountability, and freedom. Choice allows the family to select the charter school that best meets their child's needs. Accountability requires that charter school to meet the terms of their "contract" or face school closure. Freedom within the structure of a charter school allows the charter school to be free from some procedural "hoops," while still adhering to the same major laws, standards, and regulations of other public schools.

Recent data indicate that there are approximately 4,100 charter schools serving 1.2 million children across forty states and the District of Columbia. The popularity of charter schools is due to several factors, including proven quality, stronger and safer communities (especially in inner-city schools), and perhaps the major reason, that the focus of the school is on the needs of the students and the commitment to do whatever it takes for the students to succeed. The Center for Education Reform reports data from every state and also provides the locations of charter schools across the nation.

Given this information, in many ways charter schools may appear to be a perfect fit for any parent who wants to stay in the public school system, yet needs a different approach. Not all charter schools have a homeschooling component; however, some charter schools focus exclusively on the homeschool. The service delivery of the charter homeschool varies widely. Some offer no time on a school campus and weekly appointments with homeschool teachers. Some charter schools may offer site-based electives or academic classes that can supplement what the student is doing at home. Some charter homeschools develop what they call a "Personalized Learning Plan" (PLP). This plan outlines a schedule of individualized learning activities designed to meet the student's needs. Some examples of PLP activities are: a class on a public school campus along with community experiences, work with homeschool teachers, field trips, social events, participation in sports, as well as independent work at home.

Private Belief-Based

For some families the decision to homeschool their children is a belief-based decision. Regardless of the specific religious or philosophical belief, the parents making this choice often feel that they can best instruct their children in their spiritual and moral values by infusing these values in the educational structure that they provide at home. Some families of children with ASD may find the belief-based component is an essential element in homeschooling their child. Because belief-based programs are considered to be "private schools," parents choosing this option take on the responsibility of all teaching, supports, and services for their child. In other words, the public school has no obligation to provide the designated instructional services (DIS) or therapies that may be outlined in the IEP once a parent selects private education. The legal obligations of the public school are further clarified in Question 9.

The following resources provide information and curriculum related to belief-based home education. Although these resources are not designed for working with children who have ASD, they might be helpful as a basis for families seeking to have a belief-based foundation for homeschooling their child who has ASD.

Christian

Abeka: www.abeka.org

Alpha Omega: www.aop.com/home/

Bob Jones University Press: www.bjup.com

Liberty Academy School System: www.homeschools.org

Catholic

Catholic Heritage Curricula: www.chcweb.com

The Catholic Home School Network of America: www.geocities.com/Heartland/8579/chsna.html

Kolbe Academy: www.kolbe.org/storefront-c0.html

The Grace Academy for Online Homeschooling: www.thegraceacademy.org

Seton School: www.setonhome.org

Islamic

ArabesQ: www.arabesq.com

Islamic School: www.islamicschool.net

Muslim Homeschool: www.muslimhomeschool.com

Jewish

A.R.E. Publishing: www.arepublish.com

Behrman House Publishers and booksellers: www.behrmanhouse.com

Bnos Henya Project: www.bnoshenya.org

Jewish Home Educators Network: www.snj.com/jhen

Torah Aura Productions: www.torahaura.com

Latter-Day Saints

Latter-Day Saints Home Educators Association: www.ldshea.org

LDS Homeschooling Organization: www.ldshomeschooling.org

Native Americans

Native American Homeschool Association: www.mo-biz.com/~mvha/NativeAmericanHomeschoolers.html

Seventh Day Adventist

Griggs University International: www.hsi.edu/

Private Umbrella and Satellite Schools

The terms *umbrella* and *satellite* are used to describe homeschool programs that are established under another, typically private or alternative school, for families who do not feel comfortable homeschooling on their own or just want some ongoing support. Some of these schools are belief-based, but others are not. There is a fee for the type of service the umbrella or satellite school provides. The services that may be provided include curriculum guidance, materials, testing services, record keeping, high-school transcripts, and accredited diplomas.

To locate an umbrella or satellite school that supports home-schooling, contact private or faith-based schools or your local school district.

Private Cooperatives

Cooperatives are usually created by parents who have similar goals and wish to work together as a group expanding on the basic homeschooling of their children. They may select or elect a leader-ship team to coordinate programs or activities to support one another and their children. The cooperative may arrange field trips or other activities for the students, parents, or entire families. Cooperatives may charge a regular monthly fee or an occasional fee to cover materials for a special event. Typically parents commit to volunteer time throughout the year. This time might involve teaching a subject that the parent is strong in or organizing instruc-tion on a topic through a community resource such as a museum, naturalist, or art gallery. Cooperative members typically take turns hosting events or lessons at their different homes or using space in community buildings such as churches or recreation facilities. The cooperative attempts to provide structured and scheduled activities that meet the needs of both the students and the parents; thus, open communication and collaboration are keys to the success of the cooperative.

Private Correspondence or Distance Learning Programs

These types of programs are classified as "private schools." Parents must inquire about tuition or a fee for services, which varies based on the provider and sometimes the grade of the student. It is also critical that parents ensure that the program is fully accredited in preparation for transition to college, business, or trade school.

A student involved in a correspondence or distance education program typically receives a curriculum through the mail or via the computer. The student is expected to learn the material, complete the assignments, and then return the lessons to be reviewed and graded. The program provider maintains the student records, lesson planning, and verification of progress.

The use of the Internet to provide educational opportunities is growing in interest and acceptance at many levels of education. This is sometimes called "virtual school" or "cyber school." Students can be connected online and communicate with teachers, as well as other students using e-mail. Although they may be studying at home, they are connected to others. Many existing correspondence schools are including the Internet in their programs.

Parents must carefully consider the learning style of their child, as these types of programs require a degree of study on one's own, sustained attention to task, computer or writing skills, self-initiation, and responsibility. For some this may be a perfect match, whereas for others it may not fit their learning style.

Because lessons are already preplanned in a virtual-school format, parents often find they have more time to provide direct support to their child. Parents and students may find that supplementing the basic curriculum is desirable. Many correspondence or distance learning programs recommend extracurricular activities and community experiences.

Resources

The Distance Learning Resource Network's Web site http://www .dlrn.org/virtual.html is a place parents can use to start their research for online educational options. The following is a short list of correspondence or distance learning schools that are presented in alphabetical order. Virtual interactive schools have an asterisk (*).

American School: www.americanschoolofcorr.com

Babbage Net School*: www.babbagenetschool.com/

Cambridge Academy: www.cambridgeacademy.com

Chrysalis School: www.chrysalis-school.com

Citizen School: www.citizenschools.org/

Clonlara School: www.clonlara.org

CompuHigh Online*: www.compuhigh.com

Florida Virtual School*: www.flvs.net/

Francis Virtual School*: www.francisvirtualschool.org

International High School: www.internationalhigh.org

Laurel Springs: www.laurelsprings.com

Moore Academy: www.moorefoundation.com/

Oak Meadow: www.oakmeadow.com/

Online K12 homeschool program*: www.k12.com/

Sea Scape Educational Center: www.seascapecenter.com

Texas Virtual School*: www.texasvirtualschool.org/

Long-Distance Learning

Institutions of higher learning exist that provide options for homeschooling that may be considerations for some families. The following list provides families with a few sites to research:

Stanford University

Education Program for Gifted Youth (EPGY)
(kindergarten through advanced undergraduate)

Ventura Hall

Stanford University

Stanford, CA USA 94305-4115

(800) 372-EPGY

http://epgy.stanford.edu

Texas Tech K–12 Options

Outreach and Extended Studies

Texas Tech University

P.O. Box 42191

Lubbock, TX USA 79409-2191

(800) MY-COURSE (catalogue request)

University of Nebraska–Lincoln

Independent Study High School

P.O. Box 839400

Lincoln, NE USA 68583-9400

(402) 472-2175

Eclectic Schooling

When families are using components of many of the programs described above, they are practicing an eclectic approach. This combination allows families to be very creative and truly address the unique needs of their child and their personal teaching style and level of confidence. For families homeschooling a child with ASD, the eclectic approach gives them the latitude to incorporate the child's passions and interests into the curriculum on a consistent basis. For many, this is the best of all worlds.

5 | How Do Parents Choose the Right Type of Homeschool Program for Their Child?

There are two elements parents must consider when making this decision. First, they must consider the learning style of their child. It is often the learning style and needs of the child with ASD that have influenced the decision to homeschool in the first place. Second, the parents must consider their personal teaching style. Although it is typically only one parent who is the designated teacher, homeschooling is really a family endeavor. Homeschooling might be described as a new type of lifestyle that affects the entire family.

To understand the learning needs and style of the child, the parent must clearly understand the complexities of ASD as discussed in the answer to Question 1. It has been the experience of these authors that parents are often experts on their children and typically have clear insight into the learning style of their child. Many have attended hour upon hour of conferences, workshops, or seminars on autism. Though they may need training in specific teaching procedures, most parents have a good sense of the supports required for their child to be a successful learner.

Learning Styles

People learn in various ways. The three most common learning styles are: 1) visual learners, those who learn best when additional visual information is presented to clarify what is to be learned; 2) auditory learners, those who learn best when information is presented through discussion and direct verbal information; and 3) tactile-kinesthetic learners, those who learn best through active hands-on instruction and participation. To assess your child's learning style, many resources and inventories are available on the Web. Surveys and inventories to assess teaching styles are also available.

Dr. Temple Grandin, an adult woman with autism and author of the 1995 book *Thinking in Pictures,* along with other experts (Hodgdon, 1996; Cohen and Sloan, 2007; Snaver and Smith Myles, 2000) in the field of Autism Spectrum Disorders acknowledge that most individuals with ASD are visual learners.[1] Recognizing the learning style provides parents with information to assist in selecting the best type of program. It must also be acknowledged that instruction can be addressed through other modalities than the child's preferred style. Parents must look at the individual strengths, interests, and other needs of their child and what each program has to offer.

The parent must recognize his or her strengths and weaknesses as a teacher because this will influence the type of program selected. If the parent is highly organized and enjoys creating and developing curricula and materials, they may chose a more independent type of homeschooling program. If the parent has trouble with creating materials, has many time pressures that do not allow for material development, or simply does not enjoy the creative process, a more structured and prescribed program may be a good match.

Parent
Perspective

You take into account your child's strengths and weaknesses along with your own strengths and weaknesses and then venture out to find the appropriate program placement.

—Connie Ajay

One needs to consider the parent-teacher's strengths and weaknesses as well as the child's strengths and weaknesses when choosing. If the parent-teacher is not fully on board and supported in his or her role as a special education teacher, principal, bus driver, and so on; the homeschool may fail because of parent burnout.

—Karen Crum

The following scenarios give examples of what might contribute to a parent's decision to choose one type of program over another:

Scenario 1

The student enjoys certain parts of the school day, but is overwhelmed by the pace of instruction and requires more direct instruction with an expanded use of visuals. The parent is comfortable with the direct instruction, but wants to stay connected to public education for curricular support, special education services, and the opportunities to access the activities that are positive and socially based. Options that possibly meet the student and parent needs in the scenario might be a program operated by a public school such as Independent Study or a public charter school.

Parent
Perspective

My own choice was through a public charter school where I have access to resources that can support me when needed, as well as a stipend for purchasing additional instructional materials (this is one advantage of some charter school programs).

—Connie Ajay

Scenario 2

The student has been attending a private belief-based school that has met the family's philosophical focus; however, the class size, although small, is overwhelming, which results in emotional stress and frequent outbursts that are upsetting to the student and his classmates. The parent has been helping with her child's education and feels comfortable teaching, but she wants to stay connected to the families' faith and have the option to work with other families who are homeschooling their children for social activities. A belief-based private homeschool program would best meet this family's needs. If this is not available through the family's personal church, temple, or mosque, there may be other belief-based programs that correspond with their needs. Another option that might work would be to participate in a belief-based online or correspondence program while continuing social activities that already exist within the family's community church, temple, or mosque.

> ## Parent Perspective
>
> You can arrange for your child to take a few classes in a more traditional setting at a public or private school. You can have other "experts" teach your child some skills or subjects through a homeschool co-op program, or you can arrange informal or formal teaching sessions with friends, tutors, and so on.
>
> —Connie Ajay

Scenario 3

The student enjoys spending large amounts of time drawing; however, with the correct motivation, he will engage in academic activities. He also loves the computer both to play games and to research "cheats" to improve his ability to beat the games he loves. He responds well to structure and schedules, which have proven successful to reduce the anxiety he experiences with unexpected changes in his routines. His parent feels comfortable taking on the role of teacher but does not feel that any one program will meet all of his needs. Therefore, the parent concludes that an eclectic approach which incorporates a traditional-type school structure and a computer-based program will best meet his son's needs.

Scenario 4

The student was diagnosed by thirty-six months of age with ASD. He has other diagnosed disabilities, including cognitive delay and fine and gross motor delays, and at age seven years has not begun to speak. His parents feel comfortable taking on homeschooling because they participated in an in-home early intervention program from the time their son was three until he went to kindergarten. His parents chose to homeschool because they feel that they can give their son the amount of one-to-one direct instruction he requires to make progress. The parents recognize that their son's program will not focus on typical academic skills, but functional academics and life skills that will help him become as independent as possible. They also recognize that he needs therapies that are provided at the public school through his IEP. Their private insurance will also cover additional speech and language therapy. The parents and the public school recognize the unique needs and agree that an eclectic approach is required. Through the IEP process, a program is developed to support the therapy needed and provide consultation to the parents so that daily practice can occur. The parents develop a curriculum based on learning functional academics and life skills in the home. They also work with a local parent support group and an online group that offers ideas for instruction. They structure the learning environment in their home to provide visual supports for learning.

6 | What Are the Reported Advantages of Homeschooling Children with ASD?

Homeschooling a child with ASD is only one option along a continuum of options that parents may consider. Any option presents both disadvantages and advantages. Parents have reported that there are many advantages to homeschooling this population of learner. In general, homeschooling allows a parent to truly individualize instruction within a functional context that promotes generalization of skills. The parent may custom design a learning environment that meets both the learning and sensory needs of the child. Homeschooling allows parents the opportunity to provide and set up social situations that have the highest likelihood of success. It also allows for the child's special talents and interests to be incorporated and highlighted rather than viewed as a problem that interferes with learning. In this section we will explore the many advantages of homeschooling and suggest ways of capturing these in your homeschooling program.

Advantage 1: Incorporating the child's interests and tapping into the motivation to learn. Because children with ASD are "differently motivated" (not unmotivated) and do not respond in the same way to the generalized social rewards utilized in traditional educational settings, homeschooling provides a huge advantage in the area of creating and enhancing motivation. Because the child's homeschooling program is completely individualized and not locked

Parent Perspective

Homeschool allows you to think outside the box. It lends itself to accommodating a student's learning style and timeline. The whole point of education is to learn. I think teachers, parents, and students forget that. We are so busy competing and zooming through classes that we think the whole point is to fit into the school system and get good grades. For kids who don't fit into the regular school system, it is nice to be able to expand or contract the time so that they can get some real learning done and still be considered successful. There is no point in pushing them through when they aren't getting it. It just makes them feel like a failure.

—Ann Coe

Parent Perspective

Areas of interest can be woven throughout the curriculum, even if you are following prescribed grade-level standards. Reading and writing objectives can be met through child-selected topics. Field trips and art projects can revolve around interests. If science is a passion, much of the curriculum can be science-based. A child's favorite toys can be used in math and creative writing. Whatever the interest is, it can be incorporated into home instruction much easier than in the traditional classroom setting.

—Janelle Lewis

into any specific textbook or predesignated curriculum, this allows the parent-teacher to use the child's natural interests to teach many skills and concepts.

The interests can be infused in the instruction, rather than seen as interfering with the implementation of a predesigned curriculum. The student's area of special interest can actually serve as the foundation of an assignment. Examples of this are provided in Question 14.

Advantage 2: The parent can teach to the core deficits of the disability and incorporate strengths in the instructional strategies used. Homeschooling allows the parent-teacher to address the core challenges faced by the student with ASD on an ongoing basis and within many functional contexts. Working on effective communication, social skills, and social interpretation can be infused in almost every interaction and activity. Following an outing, the child can reflect on the interactions he had with others and be coached on the social understanding and perspective taking needed to have good social relations. Play skills or games can be pretaught in a highly structured and distraction-free environment and then can be generalized into more social and active situations like playgroups or other preplanned social situations.

Organizational skills and planning can be taught within each activity or daily routine. The child can learn to break down a task into manageable chunks, identify needed materials, prepare a checklist for task completion, initiate and finish the task at his pace, and see and enjoy the outcome of his actions without the time pressures or limitations of a rigid schedule or curriculum.

Visual teaching strategies and real-world learning contexts are critical instructional elements to include for students with ASD. Additionally, children with ASD tend to have learning strengths, including their ability to memorize, follow rules and procedures, and focus their attention, in distraction-free environments, for long periods of time. In a homeschooling program, the parent-teacher is able to use the learning strengths and customize the learning contexts and teaching materials to match the child's needs regardless of a child's cognitive ability.

Parent Perspective

Homeschool also enables you to set up a more "fitted" curriculum for your child, allowing you to fill in more learning gaps that actually matter in life.
—Karen Crum

You can make social skills and life skills training part of the curriculum and get school credit. You can count private music lessons as performing arts.
—Ann Coe

Parent
Perspective

The main advantage of homeschooling for the student is one-to-one instruction. All research indicates that the best way for a student, any student, is to teach in the manner in which they learn. One-to-one attention is the best way for students with ASD to be able to modify and adapt the lesson according to their strengths and weaknesses, as well as their likes or obsessions. The ability to teach in the manner that holds their attention and focus helps them to retain the information, and the crucial component is the ability to teach a lesson and then apply it to a real-world situation and across all domains.

—Connie Ajay

Advantage 3: Individualized attention can be provided. Because the student may be the only student in the homeschool setting, or may be educated in small groups through homeschooling co-ops, there is a greater chance that the child will be given more individualized attention. Immediate assessment of understanding can take place to ensure that the child is getting the skill or concept. Teaching strategies can be changed to better support the child's learning if, in fact, the child is not grasping a concept in the original way it is presented. Behavioral indicators of frustration can be recognized earlier, and the necessary support or help can be given before it reaches a crisis level.

Many studies indicate that children with ASD tend to respond best with one-on-one, highly intensive opportunities for direct instruction. The National Research Council (2001) suggests that children with ASD receive a minimum of 25 hours per week of active engagement in functional and developmentally appropriate activities in a year-round program. A heavy emphasis should be placed on generalization of learned skills, and there should be a high level of parental involvement. All of these aspects of effective programming can be accessed through homeschooling for a child who demonstrates many or few basic skills.[2]

Advantage 4: Opportunities to generalize skills. Because many of the skills being taught in homeschooling are functional skills and lessons can be designed for immediate use in real-world contexts, generalization can be built into the program from the onset and is not as elusive as in traditional school programs. In traditional school programs, contexts are often contrived. For example, the student may be given a word problem about making change at the grocery store. This leaves the student with ASD having to imagine the scenario, which may be very challenging for some with ASD. The hope is he will see how the skill he has learned can be applied in the real world, but often this does not happen. In homeschooling, the same situation can be acted out live at the grocery store, then discussed, and then written out as a word problem to be solved. This provides a deeper level of understanding and allows the child to generalize from the real world to contrived scenarios as opposed to from contrived scenarios to the real world. Learning in a natural context is important for all children with ASD; however, it is very important for children who have ASD and cognitive delays. Ultimately, the goal is for the child to be able to use the skill in the real world, not just pass that section on a test.

Advantage 5: Environment is more appropriate for the learner. By schooling at home and in the community during planned activities and outings, there is likely to be far less sensory and social stimulation, which can allow for greater focus and attention to the task and can minimize social anxiety and problematic behavior. As reported in the National Research Council's publication *Educating Children*

> ## Parent Perspective
>
> Homeschool allows your child and your family to actually relax and enjoy life on a routine basis, instead of always engaging in the frantic and impossible race to keep up with the neurotypicals.
>
> —Karen Crum

with Autism (2001), many interventions that involve changing the schedules and curricula, rearranging the physical environment, or changing the type and nature of social groupings have been shown to be highly effective and result in decreases in a variety of maladaptive behaviors. This is a shift in viewing positive behavior supports from "changing the individual to fit the environment" to "changing the environment to fit the individual learner's needs".[3]

Advantage 6: Self-awareness and self-advocacy can be worked on in a safe and supportive learning environment. The core areas of self-awareness can be targeted, in which the child is taught to identify the sensory experiences and emotional triggers as they are occurring. Through parent-teacher coaching and support, the child can learn the language with which to label the experience as it occurs. Lessons on self-regulation can be taught without the fear of missing out on other things. While self-awareness and self-regulation can be taught in a traditional educational setting, again, the learning situations are often contrived through the use of planned curricula or teaching sessions. This is not the most effective way to reach and teach a child with ASD.

Advantage 7: Homeschooling can enhance the parent-child relationship and teach these children the true meaning of social connection.

Parent Perspective

There are myriad advantages to homeschooling, but the one that I hear voiced over and over is that homeschooling parents gain a tremendous insight into their child's feelings, interests, needs, and biorhythms when working with them at home. The level of understanding and closeness between the parent and child grows tremendously. Most report that, although homeschooling can be a demanding experience, it is rewarding and enjoyable.

—Janelle Lewis

I really enjoy having time to listen to my son's views on life, history, and science. The experience of reading the same material and then discussing it one-on-one has been great for both of us.

—Ann Coe

For most children, the first and most impressionable social bond is the one they have with their parents. Children with ASD, because of the nature of their disability, have significant delays in the development of social understanding and social relatedness. Having an opportunity to develop and continue to learn about social relationships in a highly supportive family unit provides great advantages. Social mistakes can be forgiven and repaired with family in ways that they cannot be with others. Homeschooling allows for more opportunities for this social relationship to be developed.

Advantage 8: Prevent emotional and anxiety issues commonly resulting from school failures. Unfortunately, children with ASD cannot always be protected from negative encounters with those who lack knowledge and training when in the traditional school setting. There is a great deal that needs to be done before people in the general public really understand the nature of this invisible disability. Even many professional educators lack the level of awareness and training to understand these children and their unique learning and behavioral differences. This lack of understanding results in errors and misinterpretations even by very well-intentioned people. Until there is better training, more general knowledge, and easier access to specialized supports, children with ASD will continue to be misunderstood and, as a result, may be victims of circumstance. In homeschooling, the parent is able to shelter the child from many of these encounters that can cause emotional trauma until such time as the child is able to handle these situations and has acquired self-advocacy skills. The parent is able to control and monitor social interactions and is able to provide some level of training to others about the

Parent Perspective

At home, kids with ASD can learn in a relatively stress-free environment where they can relax, enjoy themselves, become more social, and experience emotional well-being and positive development while advancing academically. Oftentimes, the traditional classroom environment is too overwhelming. Some children become extremely fearful in an environment of competitiveness where their communication, ability to attend, and physical issues add to feelings of low self-esteem, not belonging, and lack of safety. Sometimes the special education services that are in place are not an appropriate match for the child's needs, or the teacher is not prepared to handle the complexities of ASD, and that causes even more stress. School at home, even for a short interval, can be a recovery haven.

—Karen Crum

disability and the child's behavior and needs. This shelter can result in positive emotional growth, higher self-esteem, and less anxiety.

In Tony Attwood's book *Asperger's Syndrome: A Guide for Parents and Professionals,* he states, "When anxiety is extreme, full-time home tuition (homeschool) has proved successful, especially with teenagers . . . this approach can be a constructive alternative to strong medication and possible admission to a psychiatric unit."[4] For some children, the emotional benefits of homeschooling and the protection it provides can literally make or break the child's learning and behavioral success. It is a very important part of a continuum of options that must be considered for children on the Autism Spectrum.

7 | What Are the Challenges of Homeschooling Children with ASD?

Whatever the learning needs of the child are, when a parent is homeschooling their child, there will be challenges facing both of them. It is important that a parent go into homeschooling considering not only the positives but the challenges as well.

Parent Perspective

Many of the challenges of homeschooling lessen over time as the parent and child become more experienced with the process. However, one can expect that there will be many challenges.

—Karen Crum

What follows are some of the challenges that any parent homeschooling their child will probably face at one time or another.

Challenge 1: Time. School takes time whether a child is attending traditional school or is being homeschooled. The level of parental involvement in traditional school is typically greater when the child has an Autism Spectrum Disorder. Parents not only participate in required annual IEP meetings but often in additional IEP meetings, and possibly regularly scheduled informal team meetings to address ongoing issues unique to a student with ASD. Usually frequent communication is needed with staff to maintain a proactive approach. Parents may also spend a great deal of time providing informal or formal training to staff. A time demand that is unplanned and adds a great deal of stress to the parent is the phone call requesting that the parent rush to school to support their child who is experiencing behavioral challenges.

The time demands when homeschooling are somewhat different, but very intense. A parent who is homeschooling will have to commit time to organizing the curriculum and materials, planning the day, providing instruction, and keeping the entire family on course. This time commitment for one parent may mean an end to work outside the home or a significant reduction of personal time during the day.

As families consider this time commitment, they must remember that homeschooling will take more time in the early stages while setting up the curriculum and structure. This will vary based on the age of the child and the type of program a family chooses to follow. The actual amount of direct instruction is usually less than the traditional school day. This gives the parent and child time to devote to more interactive and community-based activities. However, when a parent, often the mother, is taking on the homeschooling responsibilities and also carries the typical family responsibilities, the time commitment may feel overwhelming.

Parent Perspective

The biggest challenge is getting started and figuring out how to fit home-schooling into your family's structure. Homeschooling a child with ASD is time-consuming and demanding. When I am homeschooling my child, I need to forget about multitasking and have my full attention on him and what we are doing. Even though I follow his interests and leads in much of what we are doing, there is still careful planning and preparation involved—not just with the academics, but also with behavior reinforcement schedules, social and life skills lessons, and so on. All of the outside activities require organizing and transporting. It is a full-time-plus commitment that happens in conjunction with other family and home responsibilities, and it is not for everyone. I have older children (and a husband!) who are not being homeschooled, and I need to be there for them also. The balancing act is very tough, and quite often the homeschooling parent can topple without adequate support. Finding perfect balance is the key to success.

—Janelle Lewis

For the parent the biggest challenge is the time commitment. The parent is the main source of teaching and therefore the party fully responsible for ensuring the progress of the student. This pressure can weigh heavily on the parent, oftentimes causing self-doubt or undue pressure to get the student to a level of adequacy.

—Connie Ajay

Homeschool is an education, not a duplication of public school, thus the time structure will be different even from the length of day to the length of the school year. Families may choose to follow the typical 180-school-day year with summers off; or they may plan a year-round schedule. The type of program the family is following may dictate the yearlong structure. Several examples of daily homeschool schedules are provided in Question 15.

Challenge 2: Change in the parent-child relationship. When homeschooling occurs, the child and parent move into a different relationship that requires new roles and perspectives. Not only is the parent sometimes the teacher and the child sometimes the student, they are now together twenty-four hours a day interacting in one role or another. The challenge of increased time together along with the role changes can put a strain on the relationship. On the other hand, many parents report the new relationship as a benefit to homeschooling. This was discussed in Question 6.

Given the social challenges of a child with ASD, this change in roles can be even more problematic than it is with a neurotypical child. Not all children with ASD will have difficulty shifting to homeschooling and the new role their parent is taking on, but some may. For the student who may have difficulty shifting the relationship, Olga Holland, in her 2005 book *Teaching at Home: A New Approach to Tutoring Children with Autism and Asperger Syndrome,* offers parents a creative idea. The cliché that clothes make the person was used to define her new role. Her son would try to coax her into the role of "Mom" by seeking affection, but when she was dressed in her professional clothing she simply pointed out, using her professional voice, that she was a teacher now and would go back to being his mom later (when she changed her clothes). This visually made the distinction clear to her son when she was his teacher and when she was his mom.[5]

For other parents, coping with the intensity of their child's needs may affect the homeschooling relationship. It is important for parents to acknowledge truthfully what they are able to do with their child during different stages of development.

Parent
Perspective

Homeschooling would have been more stressful on our parent-child relationship when Ian was younger. Because of the ADHD aspects of his personality, I don't think I could have handled it. Now he can focus longer and can work on his own for short periods of time.

—Ann Coe

The extensive amount of time the parent and child spend together may generate some unintended outcomes such as dependency. The parent's goal is undoubtedly to send their child out into the world someday as an independent adult. Although homeschool can certainly teach independence, the intensive close relationship may inadvertently foster dependency.

Challenge 3: Lack of support. When any family has finally made the decision to homeschool their child, they may not get much support for a variety of reasons. Add the variable of choosing to homeschool a child with ASD, the lack of support may be even more prevalent, including concerns voiced not only by family members but also by professionals.

Typically, the lack of support stems from fear of the unknown and a concern for both the parent and the child. A concerned friend or family member may think that this will be too difficult and a stress on the family overall. This may be especially true when other family members do not understand the complexities of ASD and the enormous stress the parents and child deal with in a traditional school setting. Some professionals including educators, psychologists, administrators, and physicians may be concerned that

Parent
Perspective

The parent-teacher and the child with ASD spend more time together, so the child runs the risk of becoming more dependent on the parent. A conscious effort must be made to take small steps toward independence and self-initiative. Because of the increased time together, the parent-child relationship can be wonderful at times or it can become very stressful. It helps if the child is taking some classes at the school facility or with another person as teacher. Ian has a speech therapist, a math resource special education teacher, a piano teacher, a chemistry lab teacher, and his grandmother one hour a week for English. He was also in a P.E. class for homeschoolers for a semester.

—Ann Coe

Parent
Perspective

School employees, friends, and family members are often unsupportive of what may be considered a radical approach, making the adjustment more difficult for the parent and child. The adage "If mama ain't happy, nobody is happy" can apply here. Care must be given to supporting the parent who changes their lifestyle to assist their child.

—Karen Crum

there will be little opportunity for social interaction with peers, thus limiting the development of critical social skills or possibly losing social skills. There may also be a concern that the child will go more deeply into his special interests and miss out on other curricular areas.

Challenge 4: Lack of child enthusiasm about homeschooling. Some children are very excited to begin homeschooling, whereas other children want to go to school even when it is not helping them learn or is resulting in social and emotional damage. What are parents to do?

As with anything else a parent must deal with, there is not always a clear answer. There are times as parents that a decision must be made and carried out regardless of the wishes of the child. This strategy typically works better with the younger child. However, in spite of making the final decision, it is important to try to discover why the child wants to continue going to school even though there are obvious problems. It may be that there are specific activities that the child would miss, or there may be some students that he considers friends that he will miss. These situations should be considered and efforts made to allow these relationships or activities to continue. A creative, eclectic homeschool approach might work best in this situation.

When approaching the change to homeschooling with the older child, a parent may need to visually outline the pros and cons of participating in a homeschool program. Again, the parent must try to take the perspective of the older student. Striking a compromise might be the best option. This compromise might be an agreement to explore options together, such as trying to meet other students who are homeschooling. A parent might contact a local ASD support group to determine whether there are other families who are homeschooling whose children might lend support to the concept. The final compromise might be to select an option or eclectic approach and give it a try for a designated period of time and then review the results. Whatever the outcome, the parent has taught the child a valuable lesson in negotiation and compromise.

Ultimately, the parents will have to determine if homeschooling is worth the upset, especially if the child is adamant about continuing in a traditional setting. Will forcing the issue of homeschooling mean greater stress to the family? This is another question that each family will have to answer individually. Keep in mind also that because of the nature of ASD, change is challenging and may be met with some initial resistance. Once the transition is made and the child has adjusted, the protesting may cease.

Parent Perspective

The freedom of choosing the curriculum for your child is wonderful, but can be overwhelming, as the school no longer dictates the education. The realization of the responsibility that the parent accepts in homeschooling can be frightening as well. Also, motivating a child who has been in traditional school for a number of years can be difficult at first, as the external motivators of grades and social pressure no longer exist in the homeschool setting to the same degree.

—Karen Crum

The parent has to have the gift of patience. The comfort of home and all of the distractions of being at home can be tough. For example, telephone, TV, playstation, the student wanting to sleep until 10:00 in the morning, all create distractions. It's very easy to get out of the school routine when you are on your own clock.

—Michelle King

Challenge 5: Self-doubt. Even the most confident parent may experience some level of self-doubt over some component of their homeschooling plan. Typically, parents doubt their ability to do the job well, from selecting the curriculum to the best strategies to use that will be effective with their child. They may be concerned that they will have difficulty maintaining a productive routine at home and may lack the patience to keep their child learning and motivated. Some parents who choose to homeschool are credentialed teachers, but many are not.

Although these doubts are natural, the parents of children with ASD must have confidence in their innate expertise because they have learned the unique characteristics of their child since the day he was born. Most of the professional educators in traditional schools do not have the intensive training in ASD that the parent of a child with ASD has. The parent was the first and most significant

Parent Perspective

Often the child with ASD can be challenging to instruct in some areas, with fear and aversion to certain activities inherent in the diagnosis. This means that the person who commits to homeschooling is usually beginning a task in which challenges and setbacks are inherent.

There may also be behavioral problems and avoidance of the subjects that were difficult in the traditional school setting that may continue or initially worsen in the home setting where the child feels safe. However, these will lessen as the reasons for the frustrations are identified and can be addressed.

—Karen Crum

teacher, helping their child learn many basic life skills. The parent is now choosing to teach some subject matter that is usually taught at school, but the same skill, innate instincts, and persistence that have worked with other skills can be applied to these new areas as well.

The parents must remember that they are the experts on the unique needs of their child. For the parent who has self-doubts, selecting a homeschool model that has support built-in is likely a good choice in the beginning.

Challenge 6: Accessing therapies and services. A family's ability to access therapies and services will be affected by the type of home-school option they choose. Students living in the United States who have been in public school, were found eligible for special education service, and have been receiving services and support may still receive some of those services if the parents are home-schooling through a public or private charter homeschool program. Speech therapy is often continued with the parent bringing the child to a designated site for the therapy. In some public or charter homeschool programs, the children come to school on designated days each week to have classes, meet with teachers, and participate in electives and therapy as designated in their Individual Education Plan (IEP).

When parents choose an option that removes the child from public education, often the special therapies and services are dis-continued. Parents who enroll their child in a private school may seek an Individual Service Plan through the local school district in which they reside. This is not an IEP and simply outlines minimal supports up to a certain dollar amount per year. These supports typically include consultation and occasionally assessment. This is discussed in further detail in Question 9.

Some parents who have chosen to manage their child's education independently have been able to access therapy for their child through the family's medical insurance plan. The availability of these services varies across health care providers. Many families have reported that, with persistence, they have been successful in getting the health plan to cover speech therapy and occupational therapy. Sometimes, just the bureaucracy of such agencies can be daunting, but with perseverance it may be a viable option for families to pursue.

There are also parents who feel the progress they are making in the education of their child is more valuable than the therapy that was available through any other option. As with all decisions surrounding homeschooling a child, it is ultimately the parent's decision what the program will include. If accessing therapy is a challenge, there are many creative options that parents can explore.

Challenge 7: Knowing and understanding the laws and regulations. Knowing, understanding, and following the laws and regulations regarding homeschooling requirements is critical to parents who are choosing to homeschool their child. Laws vary from state to state. So a parent who has been homeschooling in California and moves to Minnesota must research the prevailing laws and regulations. However, in the United States homeschooling is legal in all fifty states. In fact, our research indicates that homeschooling is legal in many countries, including Canada, England, Ireland, Australia, and New Zealand.

The Internet has proven to be a good way to access individual state laws regarding homeschooling. A parent must then research at the local level and contact their school district to understand how the state laws have been interpreted and are being implemented locally. Parents may also want to contact a local homeschool group to gain other parents' perspectives on how to navigate the local system. A resource for finding a local homeschool group is www .homeschool.com/groups. Making contact with parent support groups for ASD or other special needs may also be helpful.

Sound advice from an educator and legal counsel is to keep thorough written records related to your homeschool program. Meet deadlines for paperwork; in fact, be early if possible. The only way anyone can maintain and prove the quality of his work is through excellent documentation. Good documentation can prevent problems in the future and provide invaluable information when it is time for transition to the next step or program.

Challenge 8: The cost of homeschooling. Concerns about funding and the costs associated with homeschooling may influence the parent's decision regarding the type of program they choose. Some families may even initially think they cannot afford to homeschool their child. Research conducted by the National Home Education Research Institute (NHERI) concluded that the average amount spent annually on a neurotypical student averaged about $450. A survey conducted on the Web showed great variation in responses ranging from next to nothing to several thousand dollars per year. When considering these amounts, one must recognize that these costs may include such things as music lessons that the child would have taken regardless of his school program. Families who are educating a child with ASD must acknowledge that there may be additional expenses for therapies or specific interventions; however, the costs can be creatively minimized.

Parents often question how they will purchase all the curricula and materials needed to appropriately educate their child at home. If a parent has chosen a public or charter homeschool program, materials should be provided at no cost. Costs in public homeschool programs should be similar to any other public school, covering only extra activities and materials. Parents may spend more in the initial setup of the homeschooling program because they are enthusiastic and possibly haven't found the low-cost and free resources that are accessible. If instructional materials are not available through the program that was chosen, there are free or low-cost materials that may be accessed. The public library is a wonderful free resource for many things. Other resources can be found by using Internet search engines and typing in keywords such as "free educational materials" or "low-cost teaching materials." Other low-cost options include shopping at some teacher supply stores that give a "teacher discount" to parents who are homeschooling. Some cooperative homeschool groups buy supplies in bulk and pass the savings on to everyone in the group. Some state homeschool organizations hold curriculum fairs once or twice a year selling used books, software, and supplies.

Setting a budget is a way to establish guidelines to limit spending. Involving the child in setting a budget and ordering supplies can be motivating and provide a feeling of ownership. Shopping at discount or consignment stores is a way to get materials and equipment at a lower cost. The instructional materials, whether new or used, may require either accommodations or modifications for the student with ASD, but most parents of these children have been doing this for years (it is often a reason that they have chosen to homeschool), so this may not be seen as a drawback.

Some Web sites may charge a membership fee, but do provide resources for free or offer low-cost materials. The following resource list should be checked out:

www.edhelper.com: Membership fee required.

www.abcteach.com: There are free printable games and activities, unit studies, research projects, and more; or one can join for other materials.

The general expense of the homeschool program is only one of the costs that parents must consider. For some families, implementing a homeschool program means that one parent will need to take on the administration, daily instruction, and supervision of the child who is now home full-time. If this parent, typically the mother, is not already staying at home to manage the home and family, there will be a loss of income. This is not a decision families can take lightly because it requires a change in lifestyle. Some parents have been able to shift to part-time employment or have been able to work from home and successfully manage to home-school their child. Other families choose to leave employment completely, dedicating their entire day to educating their child in both formal and informal ways.

Most families agree that the sacrifices have been more than worth it on many levels, including bringing families together and reducing other stresses they were living with on a daily basis. Homeschool does not need to be expensive to be a positive experience when a family is creative with the choices they make.

Parent Perspective

Unfortunately, one of the challenges of homeschooling is financial. Even at the high-school level, I must be there to keep Ian on task, so our family must forfeit one paycheck.

—Ann Coe

The parent who takes on the responsibility of homeschooling may give up his or her career and/or much of his or her free or personal time to commit to directing the education of the child. Depending on the personality, education, and resources of the parent, issues such as depression, confusion, fear, and feelings of inadequacy can be formidable to overcome.

—Karen Crum

Challenge 9: Burnout. Although most parents find homeschooling their child to be very rewarding, they also state that it can be exhausting too. This exhaustion can lead to parents feeling "burned out" and possibly questioning their ability to continue on with the demand of homeschooling their child. Two factors that are mentioned most frequently as issues leading to burnout are, first, a lack of personal time, and second, maintaining a patient attitude on a daily basis. The parent who is taking on the role of homeschool teacher now has no break from the demands of being the parent and the teacher. This situation is usually more pronounced when homeschooling younger children who may not sustain independent activities for very long. Students in upper grades tend to sustain more independent focus on their studies; thus, a parent's guidance may be required less frequently. Of course, this will vary from student to student.

The first word of advice is not to be too hard on yourself and know from the start that there will be some difficult days. Acknowledge that homeschooling will be more difficult in the beginning, but will get easier as you and your child develop a structure and rhythm that suits you both.

Parent Perspective

The child and the parent spend a great deal of time together, and this can cause a strain on the relationship. It is crucial that the child and parent find ways to spend time away from one another.

—Connie Ajay

To be able to handle the demands of homeschooling, parents must first take care of their personal stress level. This may be easier said than done. The parent-teacher may need to schedule some time away from the child to recharge. If this is difficult to schedule with family support, it can be arranged by trading student support time with other parents who are homeschooling. Families may also schedule time at a recreation center or YMCA that offers a child recreation group that does not require parent participation. While the child is engaged in a program, the parent can have time to relax, take a walk, or find a nice spot to read or just sit and enjoy the peace and quiet.

Some parents have reported that online chat groups for home-schoolers help to rejuvenate their morale and enthusiasm. Others have suggested that reading the stories of other families who are homeschooling can inspire them. Although there are not many books or Web sites specifically for those families who are home-schooling children with ASD, other homeschooling resources can prove to be supportive as well because the general challenges of homeschooling any child are similar.

3

Questions About Resources for Homeschoolers

| 8 | What Supports, Resources, and Curricula Are Available and How Can Families Access Them? |

Supports for Homeschool Families

Developing a "support network" is critical in the beginning just to get started on this journey. This network is also critical for the seasoned veteran for ongoing support and new ideas. Each family's network of supports should be customized to meet their unique needs. Families are encouraged to seek local support; however, they should also recognize that the Internet has opened the world to establishing a national or international network of support. As homeschooling becomes a part of the continuum of educational options for students with ASD, more support should become available.

Parent Perspective

Parents can start their own support group, or they can seek out other families in their area who homeschool their children. I have found that most families who homeschool their children are very diverse and quite accepting.

—Connie Ajay

Many communities have homeschooling networks that have online forums as well as live community gatherings, support groups, and co-ops to join. There are many opportunities for homeschool children to meet, play, and socialize, as well as time for the parents to swap ideas and information. For example, some group educational/social activities in my area include a homeschooling Bible study for moms, which also provides children's activities. There are homeschool park days, roller-skating days, P.E. classes, writing classes, science clubs, book clubs, theater productions, snow ski trips, and field trips ranging from a radio station tour to a day at an animal rescue farm to tours of the state capital building. A good way to find out about local resources is by gathering with other homeschooling parents and attending homeschooling conferences.

—Karen Crum

Homeschool family support networks may be available in the community. An initial search for local homeschool programs or supports can begin online or in the yellow pages of the phone book. A few calls may give a family a place to start. Local support may also come from the public schools if the family has chosen to participate in a public or public charter homeschool program. Besides the teacher with whom the family is working, a speech pathologist, program specialist, or psychologist may also be a good source of support and information. The family may also find support from private counselors or therapists.

Internet homeschooling Web sites that offer support and resources are increasing in number. The Web has become an amazing resource for almost anything a parent could want regarding homeschooling their child. The following list of sites that are specific for families who homeschool their students with ASD may provide help to beginning and veteran families.

Online Support Groups for Homeschooling Children with ASD

Asperger's Homeschool: http://groups.yahoo.com/group/Aspergers Homeschool/

Parents who homeschool a child with Asperger's Syndrome, high functioning autism, or perhaps another similar disorder may join this group to talk about what helps, what doesn't, or just to get some support from people who understand homeschooling a child with ASD.

Aut-2B-Home: www.weirdkids.com/autism/aut2bhome.htm

This is a private e-mail list of families who are homeschooling their children with autism either full-time or part-time. The members discuss education and autism, as well as how to develop programs that meet individual needs and learning styles, teaching methods, curriculums, resources, and many more topics.

FAQs On Homeschooling Special Needs: www.almadenvalleychris tianschool.com/FAQs.htm

Sharon Hensley is an educational consultant who is homeschooling her three children, including her daughter with autism.

Homeschooling Kids with Disabilities: http://groups.yahoo.com/ group/hkwd/

This is a private e-mail list of families of children with various disabilities who are homeschooling their children full- or part-time.

Connections to families of children with ASD may be made through this link.

Tammy Glaser, Founder of Aut-2B-Home: home.earthlink.net/~tammyglaser798/authome.html

This Web site not only tells one family's story of homeschooling their children, it also provides many valuable links to other information about autism and homeschooling. This is definitely a site to investigate.

OASIA (Online Asperger Syndrome Information and Support): www.udel.edu/bkirby/asperger/

This is a comprehensive information Web site for families of children diagnosed with Asperger Syndrome (AS) and related disorders, educators who teach children with AS, professionals working with individuals diagnosed with AS, and individuals with AS who are seeking support.

Parents Rearing and Educating Autistic Children in Christian Homes (PREACCH): http://groups.yahoo.com/group/PREACCH/

This is an e-mail group that was organized to encourage and support those who have decided to educate their autistic child in their home. Membership is restricted to those who will agree to pray for other members and to honor the privacy of others' comments, questions, and testimonies. Membership is also restricted to Christians.

Books Related to Homeschooling Students with ASD

Dowty, T., and Cowlishaw, K. *Home Educating Our Autistic Spectrum Children: Paths Are Made by Walking.* London: Jessica Kingsley Publishers, 2002.

Hartnett, M. K. *Choosing Home: Deciding to Homeschool with Asperger's Syndrome.* London: Jessica Kingsley Publishers, 2004.

Holland, O. *Teaching at Home: A New Approach to Tutoring Children with Autism and Asperger Syndrome.* London: Jessica Kingsley Publishers, 2005.

Pyles, L. *Hitchhiking Through Asperger Syndrome*. London: Jessica Kingsley Publishers, 2002.

Pyles, L. *Homeschooling the Child with Asperger Syndrome: Real Help for Parents Anywhere and on Any Budget*. London: Jessica Kingsley Publishers, 2004.

General Homeschooling Resources

Books

Bell, D. *The Ultimate Guide to Homeschooling*, Nashville, TN: Tommy Nelson, 2001.

Davis, M. *So—Why Do You Homeschool? Answering Questions People Ask About Home Education*. USA: Xulon Press, 2005.

Dobson, L. *The Homeschooling Book of Answers: 88 Important Questions Answered by Homeschooling's Most Respected Voices*. Rocklin, CA: Prima Publishing, 1998.

Field, C. *Help for the Harried Homeschooler: A Practical Guide to Balancing Your Child's Education with the Rest of Your Life*. Colorado Springs, CO: Water Brooks Press, 2002.

Ishizuka, K. *The Unofficial Guide to Homeschooling*. Foster City, CA: IDG Books Worldwide, 2000.

McIntire, D. *Home Schooling: Answers to Questions Parents Most Often Ask*. Huntington Beach, CA: Creative Teaching Press, 1995.

Web Sites

Home School Legal Defense Associate (HSLDA): www.hslda.org

This Web site provides current legal information on homeschool issues both nationally and internationally.

Jon's Homeschool Resource Page: www.midnightbeach.com/hs/

This is a neutral noncommercial site created by a homeschooling Dad and features quick tips, frequently asked questions, support group contacts, and teaching ideas.

The National Home Education Network (NHEN): www.nhen.org
National Home Education Network
P.O. Box 41067
Long Beach, CA 90853
Fax: (561) 581-1463

The National Home Education Network exists to encourage and facilitate the vital grassroots work of state and local homeschooling organizations and individuals by providing information, fostering networking, and promoting public relations on a national level.

National Home Education Research Institute: www.nheri.org

NHERI is a key international leader specializing in homeschool research (home-education research).

Resources for Homeschooling Students with Other Disabilities

Books

Armstrong, T. *In Their Own Way: Discovering and Encouraging Your Child's Personal Learning Style.* New York: Putnam, 1988.

Greene, R. *The Explosive Child: A New Approach for Understanding and Parenting Easily Frustrated, "Chronically Inflexible" Children.* New York: HarperCollins Publishers, 1998. www.explosivechild.com/books

Hertzog, J. *Learning in Spite of Labels.* Alhambra, CA: Green Leaf Press, 1994.

Sutton, J. *Strategies for Struggling Learners.* Simpsonville, SC: Exceptional Diagnostics, 1995.

Web Sites

A to Z Home's Cool: Homeschooling Special Needs: www.gomilpitas.com/homeschooling/weblinks/specialneeds.htm

This site can be a guide to the best, most interesting, and useful sites and articles about homeschooling on the Web. Type in "autism" and link to many very interesting sites, including those created by adults with ASD.

All Kinds of Minds: www.allkindsofminds.org

The Web site of Dr. Mel Levine, author of *The Myth of Laziness,* offers help for students who struggle with learning.

BayShore Educational: Homeschooling Special Needs Resources: www.bayshoreeducational.com/special.html

This site was developed by a homeschooling mother to offer updated resources to families who are considering or are already involved in homeschool.

CA-HEAL: California Home Education for Alternative Learners (CA-HEAL): http://groups.yahoo.com/group/CA-HEAL

This is an e-mail list of California families who are (or who are interested in) homeschooling their special needs children.

Computers for Handicapped Independence Program: http://polio.dyndns.org/chip/index.html

This site provides information on software and hardware for persons with varied limitations in motor, vision, learning, hearing, or cognitive skills.

Davis Dyslexia Correction: www.dyslexia.com

Tools to overcome problems with reading, writing, and attention focus. (888) 999-3324.

Exceptional Diagnostics: www.edtesting.com

Joe Sutton, Ph.D., offers an online software program link for creating the most appropriate instructional accommodations. A fee is charged for this service.

Finding Positive Support for Challenges: www.hsc.org/gateway/inted15.html

This site provides links to a variety of good special needs Web sites.

Homeschooling Children with Special Needs: www.geocities.com/athens/8259/special/html

This is an extensive list of special needs resources that covers everything from defining homeschool to networking and support.

Parents can also find help with lesson plans, testing, and curricula. This site has it all.

kaleidoscope.com: www.kaleidoscope.com

This is an information and resource portal for many topics. Type in an area of interest such as special needs, autism, homeschooling, and so on, and find many interesting links to follow.

NATHHAN: National Challenged Homeschoolers Associated Network: www.nathhan.com

This is a Web site for Christian families homeschooling special needs children. 5383 Alpine Rd. SE, Olalla, WA 98359, (208) 267-6246.

Recorded Books: www.recordedbooks.com

Thousands of unabridged titles by favorite authors, narrated by critically acclaimed actors, are available to check out. (800) 638-1304.

Recording for the Blind & Dyslexic: www.rfbd.org

This is a nonprofit support for those with documented visual impairment, learning disability, or other physical disability that makes reading standard print difficult or impossible. (800) 221-4792.

Sensory Processing Disorder Network: www.spdfoundation.net

Resources and information about Sensory Integration are available at this site.

General Information About Autism and Asperger's Syndrome

Autism Education Foundation: www.autismlessons.org

The purpose of the Autism Education Foundation is to make high-quality teaching materials on autism available to college instructors, high school teachers, and other educators. You are encouraged to adapt the materials to your specific needs.

Autism Resources Page: www.autism-resources.com/I

This site provides information and links regarding the developmental disabilities autism and Asperger's Syndrome.

Autism Organizations Worldwide: www.autism-india.org/worldorgs.html

This site provides links to support and information on autism around the world.

California Legislative Blue Ribbon Commission on Autism: http://senweb03.senate.ca.gov/autism/index.html

This Web site outlines California's efforts to address the needs of individuals with autism with a sixteen-member Commission representing parents of children with autism, the public and private sector, educators, physicians, and public health officials.

Tony Attwood: www.tonyattwood.com.au

Internationally renowned author and lecturer Tony Attwood offers information, publications, links, support groups, research, and much more.

Wendy Lawson's Home Page: www.mugsy.org/wendy/index.htm

Wendy is an adult woman with autism who offers insightful information to the reader as well as other resources. This is definitely worth a visit.

Accessing Curriculum

As Terri Dowty states in the introduction to her book *Home Educating Our Autistic Spectrum Children: Paths Are Made by Walking,* "There is no 'home education curriculum,' no user manual."[1] Each family must develop the curriculum that works best for them. The curriculum grows from a personal family vision that will probably look nothing like any other program. The following ideas and resources will assist parents to access the basic curriculum areas.

If parents have chosen to work with a public or public charter homeschool program, basic curricular materials are often loaned to the parents. The following is a short list of suppliers who offer

Parent Perspective

Some programs provide textbooks and materials via a credentialed supervising teacher who maps out and helps plan delivery of the curriculum. Many home study offices have a curriculum library that parents can access. There are programs that offer parents a stipend to purchase their own curricular materials, either online or from teacher supply stores. Lots of free lesson and unit ideas are available online, and the best free curriculum resource of all is the public library. Books that are full of teaching ideas are available at any bookstore. Attending a homeschooling conference can send parents home with a tremendous amount of teaching resources. Parents wanting to keep their child's educational objectives in line with what other public school students are learning should visit their State Department of Education's Web site to access the academic standards and reading lists for their child's grade level. Many school districts have pacing charts and a wealth of curricular ideas available on their Web sites. In this information age, accessing curriculum never seems to be the problem; choosing from the wealth of options is the hard part.

—Janelle Lewis

secular curriculum materials. Resources that are belief-based were provided in Chapter Two, Question 4.

Core Curriculum of America: www.core-curriculum.com

Curriculum Services: www.curriculumservices.com

K–12 Curriculum: www.curriculumservices.com

Laurelwood Books: www.laurelwoodbooks.com

The Back Pack: www.thebackpack.com

The Educator's Exchange: www.edexbooks.com

Parent Perspective

There are online classes that are available for a fee. Sometimes these online classes may be paid by your local school district. Also available for various prices are "school in a box" kits available for those who feel they need very clearly defined assignments and traditional textbooks with everything already preplanned. There are video lectures that cover many subjects so your child could have a "DVD teacher" for some subjects. There are even online writing tutors who will give your child assignments and feedback on their writing via e-mail.

—Karen Crum

Although basic curriculum areas such as language arts, math, science, and social studies often form the foundation for a homeschool curriculum, the family may have other curriculum goals as well. They may want to focus on certain life skills, values, and ethics. A family homeschooling a child with ASD may want to focus more instructional time on the core deficit areas, thus developing a curriculum around life skills, social skills, inferential thinking, problem solving, understanding figurative language, emotional regulation, and executive functioning skills. The following curricular resources specific to students with ASD have proven to be useful in both home and school settings by educators and parents. These books are listed by categories that require special instructional attention when teaching a child with ASD either in a school setting or at home. Additional resources cited in this book are listed in the Additional Resources section at the end of the book.

Instructional Strategies

Cohen, M., and Sloan, D. *Visual Supports for People with Autism: A Guide for Parents and Professionals.* Bethesda, MD: Woodbine House, 2007.

McClannahan, L., and Krantz, P. *Activity Schedules for Children with Autism: Teaching Independent Behavior.* Bethesda, MD: Woodbine House, 1999.

Mesibov. G. B., and Howley, M. *Accessing the Curriculum for Pupils with Autistic Spectrum Disorders: Using the TEACCH Programme to Help Inclusion.* London, England: David Fulton Publishers, 2003.

Mesibov. G., Shea, V., and Schopler, E. *The TEACCH Approach to Autism Spectrum Disorders.* New York: Academic/Plenum Publishers, 2005.

Socialization

Baron-Cohen, S. *Mindblindness: An Essay on Autism and Theory of Mind.* Cambridge, Mass.: MIT Press, 1997.

Cooper, B., and Widdows, N. *Knowing Yourself, Knowing Others: A Workbook for Children with Asperger's Disorder, Nonverbal Learning Disorder & Other Social-Skill Problems.* Oakland, CA: New Harbinger Publications, 2008.

Coyne, P., Nybery, C., and Vandenburg, M. *Developing Leisure Time Skills for Persons with Autism: A Practical Approach for Home, School and Community.* Arlington, TX: Future Horizons, 1999.

Duke, M. P., Nowicki, S., and Martin, E. A. *Teaching Your Child the Language of Social Success.* Atlanta, GA: Peachtree Publishers, 1996.

Garcia-Winner, M. *Think Social! A Social Thinking Curriculum for School Age Students.* San Jose, CA: Think Social Publishing, 2005. www.socialthinking.com

Garcia-Winner, M. *Worksheets for Teaching Social Thinking and Related Skills*. San Jose, CA: Think Social Publishing, 2006. www .socialthinking.com

McAfee, J. *Navigating the Social World: A Curriculum for Individuals with Asperger's Syndrome, High Functioning Autism and Related Disorders*. Arlington, TX: Future Horizons, 2002.

Moyes, R. *Incorporating Social Goals in the Classroom: A Guide for Teachers and Parents for Children with High-Functioning Autism and Asperger Syndrome*. London, UK, and Philadelphia, PA: Jessica Kingsley Publishers, 2001. www.jkp.com

Smith Myles, B., Trautman, M. L., and Schelvan, R. L. *The Hidden Curriculum: Practical Solutions for Understanding Unstated Rules in Social Situations*. Shawnee Mission, KA: Autism Asperger Publishing Company, 2004.

Wolfberg, P. *Peer Play and the Autism Spectrum: The Art of Guiding Children's Socialization and Imagination*. Shawnee Mission, KA: Autism Asperger Publishing Company, 2000.

Communication

Schuler, A. L. "Thinking in Autism: Difference in Learning and Development". In K. A. Quill (Ed.), *Teaching Children with Autism: Strategies to Enhance Communication and Socialization* (pp. 11–32). New York: Delmar, 1995.

Schwartz, S., and Miller, J. *The New Language of Toys: Teaching Communication Skills to Children with Special Needs: A Guide for Parents and Teachers*. Bethesda, MD: Woodbine House, 1996.

Behavioral Issues

Elliott, G. R. *Medicating Young Minds*. New York: Abrams, 2006. www.hnabooks.com

Smith Myles, B., and Southwick, J. *Asperger Syndrome and Difficult Moments: Practical Solutions for Tantrums, Rages and Meltdowns.* Shawnee Mission, KA: Autism Asperger Publishing Company, 2005.

Sensory and Emotional Regulation

Dunn-Buron, K. *A 5 Is Against the Law! Social Boundaries: Straight Up! An Honest Guide for Teens and Young Adults.* Shawnee Mission, KA: Autism Asperger Publishing Company, 2007.

Dunn-Buron, K., and Curtis, M. *The Incredible 5-Point Scale: Assisting Students with Autism Spectrum Disorders in Understanding Social Interactions and Controlling Their Emotional Responses.* Shawnee Mission, KA: Autism Asperger Publishing Company, 2003.

Kranowitz, C. *The Out-of-Sync Child: Recognizing and Coping with Sensory Integration Dysfunction.* New York: Perigee, 1998.

Transition Planning

Baker, J. *Preparing for Life: The Complete Guide for Transitioning to Adulthood for Those with Autism and Asperger's Syndrome.* Arlington, TX: Future Horizons, 2005.

Blackmon, D., and others. *Transition to Adult Living: An Information and Resource Guide.* Rohnert Park, CA: CalSTAT Publications, 2007.

Bolick, T. *Asperger Syndrome and Adolescence: Helping Preteens and Teens Get Ready for the Real World.* Gloucester, MA: Fair Winds Press, 2001.

Diagnostic Center, Northern California. Transition Portfolios and Guides for Middle School and High School. www.dcn-cde.ca.gov/portfolios.htm

Division TEACCH, Treatment and Education of Autistic and Related Communication-Handicapped Children. The (NEW)

TEACCH Transition Assessment Profile (TTAP) Kit. www.teacch .com/materials.html

Harpur, J., Lawlor, M., and Fitzgerald, M. *Succeeding in College with Asperger Syndrome: A Student Guide.* London, UK: Jessica Kingsley Publishers, 2004.

Marquette, J. *Becoming Remarkably Able: Walking the Path to Talents, Interests and Personal Growth for Individuals with Autism Spectrum Disorders and Related Disabilities.* Shawnee Mission, KS: Autism Asperger Publishing Company, 2007.

Meyer, R. *Asperger Syndrome Employment Workbook.* London, UK: Jessica Kingsley Publishers, 2001.

Molloy, H., and Vasil, L. *Asperger Syndrome, Adolescence and Identity: Looking Beyond the Label.* London, UK: Jessica Kingsley Publishers, 2004.

Palmer, A. *Realizing the College Dream with Autism or Asperger Syndrome: A Parent's Guide to Student Success.* London, UK: Jessica Kingsley Publishers, 2006.

Perner, L. "Preparing to Be Nerdy Where Nerdy Can Be Cool: College Planning for the Student with High Functioning Autism." Proceedings, Autism Society of America, Indianapolis, IN: July 17–21, 2002.

Silverman, S., and Weinfeld, R. *School Success for Kids with Asperger's Syndrome.* Waco, TX: Prufrock Press, 2007.

Resources Related to Self-Awareness

Gerland, G. *Finding Out About Asperger Syndrome, High Functioning Autism and PDD.* London, UK: Jessica Kingsley Publishers, 1997.

Jackson, Luke. *Freaks, Geeks & Asperger Syndrome: A User Guide to Adolescence.* London, UK: Jessica Kingsley Publishers, 2002.

Korin, E. S. *Asperger Syndrome, An Owner's Manual: What You, Your Parents and Your Teachers Need to Know*. Shawnee Mission, KS: Autism Asperger Publishing Company, 2006.

Schnurr, R. G. *Asperger's Huh? A Child's Perspective*. Arlington, TX: Future Horizons Publishing, 1999.

Yoshida, Y. *How to Be Yourself in a World That's Different: An Asperger Syndrome Study Guide for Adolescents*. London, UK: Jessica Kingsley Publishers, 2007.

Web Site Resources for Publications and Products
Autism Asperger Publishing Company: www.asperger.net

This publishing company offers a wide variety of resources with ideas for practical application for individuals with ASD.

Autism and Behavior Training Associates Publications and Products: www.autismandbehavior.com

This site offers educator- and parent-tested products and publications that address executive functioning, social thinking, and inclusive education for students with ASD and related disorders.

CompuThera: www.computhera.com

This is a **Compu**ter-assisted **Thera**py based on applied behavior analysis (ABA) and discrete trial training (DTT) procedures designed to teach cognitive skills to children with autism and visual learners. More specifically, it is a seven-step reading software program meant to complement home or school teaching programs for children with autism.

Different Roads to Learning: www.difflearn.com (800) 853-1057

This is a catalogue of materials and books for working with children with special needs.

Future Horizons Inc.: www.futurehorizons-autism.com

The world's leading publisher of books and tapes on autism and related disorders.

Handwriting Without Tears: www.hwtears.com (301) 263-2700.

Program developed by an occupational therapist and handwriting specialist.

Lindamood-Bell: www.lindamoodbell.com

Lindamood-Bell's programs stimulate basic sensory functions related to learning and are recognized as being effective in the instruction of dyslexia, hyperlexia, autism, and learning disabilities in general. The company has many programs to address academic performance, critical thinking, study skills, and following directions. They support parents through their learning centers, schools with onsite services, and professionals through professional developments.

On-the-Same-Page: www.goenglish.com/1703.asp

This Web site offers explanations about idioms that are commonly used. It might be a helpful site when teaching these figures of speech that are often very confusing.

Pyramid Educational Products: www.pyramidproducts.com

Publisher of the Picture Exchange Communication System and the book *Pyramid Approach to Education in Autism,* plus other products to support learning.

Social Skills Builder: www.socialskillbuilder.com

Social Skill Builder software can help children rapidly improve their skills in the following areas: Appropriate Social Behavior, Interactions and Relationships, Social Emotions, and Problem-Solving, by presenting video sequences of real-life social scenarios and offering appropriate responses.

Special Needs Project: www.specialneeds.com

This site carries a large selection of books on autism and other special populations.

The Gray Center for Social Learning and Understanding: www .thegraycenter.org

This is a nonprofit organization dedicated to individuals with ASD and those who work alongside them to improve mutual understanding. They approach the social impairment in ASD as a shared impairment. The Gray Center works to improve social understanding on both sides of the social equation, helping individuals with ASD to communicate and interact more successfully with the people with whom they live and work.

Time Timer: www.timetimer.com

This company makes products that help with the concept of elapsed time. Their timers make it easier for people of all ages and ability levels to understand the passage of time. Time Timer takes the visual depiction of elapsed time and turns it into a line of products to help solve time perception problems. These timers can be used anywhere.

Ultimate Learning for Kids: www.ultimatelearning.net

This computer software series provides informational reading tasks that develop problem-solving language, thus enabling a deeper understanding of the way things work and the world around us. They are dedicated to helping children with ASD.

Resources for Children with More Severe Disabilities

When parents are homeschooling a child with ASD and severe cognitive disability, the following resources may be very helpful. These resources focus on breaking tasks down to the smaller instructional components and then linking skills together to teach the individual to either fully or partially participate in whole tasks and functional routines. The curricular focus for a child with multiple disabilities is to develop adaptive skills that will increase independence in daily living and the community.

Bondy, A., and Sulzer-Azaroff, B. *The Pyramid Approach to Education in Autism.* Newark, DE: Pyramid Educational Products, 1996.

Chassman, M. *One-on-One: Working with Low-Functioning Children with Autism and Other Developmental Disabilities.* Verona, WI: IEP Resources, 1999.

Coyne, P., Nybery, C., and Vandenburg, M. *Developing Leisure Time Skills for Persons with Autism: A Practical Approach for Home, School and Community.* Arlington, TX: Future Horizons, 1999.

Ford, A., and others. *The Syracuse Community-Referenced Curriculum Guide for Students with Moderate and Severe Disabilities.* Baltimore, MD: Paul H. Brookes Publishing, 1989.

Leaf, R., and McEachin, J. *A Work in Progress: Behavior Management Strategies and a Curriculum for Intensive Behavioral Treatment of Autism.* New York: CRL Books, 1999.

Maurice, C. *Behavioral Intervention for Young Children with Autism: A Manual for Parents and Professionals.* Austin, TX: Pro-Ed, 1996.

Lesson Planning

Once curricular goals are determined, parents need to develop lesson plans. Lesson plans simply outline what activities and materials are going to be used to teach the child the information the parent wants him to learn (see Table 3.1.). An example of a simple social studies lesson plan for a child with ASD is provided (see Table 3.2).

Table 3.1. Lesson Planning Form

Subject	
Academic Objective	
Social and /or Communication Objective	
Other Objective(s)	
Steps to Meet Objectives	
Materials	
Evaluation	

Table 3.2. Lesson Planning Form Sample

Subject	Social Studies
Academic Objective	Learn about three community helpers who are in some way involved with vehicles (this child has a high interest in vehicles).
Social and /or Communication Objective	Make appropriate social greetings and ask three informational questions and one emotional question.
Other Objective(s)	Prevocational: Explore types of jobs that involve vehicles.
Steps to Meet Objectives	Research community helpers and categorize them into two groups: 1) helpers who are involved with vehicles as part of their job; and 2) helpers who are not involved with vehicles as part of their job. Pick three helpers who are involved with vehicles as part of their job. Write a list of three factual questions and one emotional question such as "Why do you like your job?" Role-play meeting each of these helpers using appropriate social greetings and asking the questions that are written on the paper. Arrange a field trip to visit each helper. Conclude the lesson with either a written, picture, or video summary of what was learned.
Materials	Books and/or videos from the library, Internet search, paper, pencil, and video camera (if filming is determined to be part of the concluding activity).
Evaluation	Using the visual Lesson Evaluation Scale (see Table 3.3), rank the lesson Super, Great, Good, OK, or Not the Best. Both the parent and the child should evaluate the outcome. If the decision is that the project was OK or Not the Best, a plan can be made to improve upon the next lesson.

The plan also demonstrates how to intentionally address the core deficits of ASD in a relevant and meaningful way and how lessons can be built around a child's area of interest, thus ensuring more motivation on the part of the child.

The following Web sites offer some sample lesson plans of ideas for creating your own lesson plans:

Table 3.3. Lesson Evaluation Scale

This scale was completed by the ☐ student; ☐ parent	
This lesson was	**Because**
Super ☐	
Great ☐	
Good ☐	
OK ☐	
Not the Best ☐	

Ask Eric Lesson Plans: http://askeric.org/Virtual/Lessons

DiscoverySchool: www.education-world.com

Lesson Plan Search: www.lessonplansearch.com

Lesson Plans Page: www.lessonplanspage.com

LessonplanZ.com: www.lessonplanz.com

Teachers.net: http://teachers.net/lessons/

Free worksheets are available on the following Web sites:

Learning Page: www.learningpage.com

School Express: www.schoolexpress.com

Tampa Reads: www.tampareads.com

Teach-nology: http://worksheets.teach-nology.com

Free Educational Games can also be found on the Internet at these sites:

Education for Kids: www.edu4kids.com

Education Place: www.eduplace.com/edugames.html

Fun Brain: www.funbrain.com

Gamequarium: www.gamequarium.com

Kids Games: www.kidsgames.org

Owl and Mouse: www.yourchildlearns.com/owlmouse.htm

Puzzle Depot: www.puzzledepot.com

9 | What Special Education Services Is My Child Entitled to if I Choose to Homeschool?

Entitlement in Public Homeschool or Public Charter Homeschool

The answer to the question on entitlement to special education services depends on the type of homeschool program selected. If the homeschool program is a public school (oftentimes called an independent study program) or a public charter school, the child is entitled to special education services and supports as determined by the IEP team and as specified in the IEP document. Oftentimes, homeschoolers who participate in these programs will come to a public school site or educational setting to receive their designated instructional services. Some of the common services provided in this way are speech therapy,

Parent Perspective

If parents choose a public charter school, they need to speak and possibly interview the special education department, including the special education director, to see what type of knowledge and support they have about ASD.

—Connie Ajay

occupational therapy, adaptive physical education, and sometimes resource specialist supports for math or reading.

Required IEP Team Agreement

An important point for parents to remember is that the IEP team must agree to the Independent Study or Charter Homeschool program in order for the Special Education Services to be implemented. It is essential to involve the IEP team in the decision making and make very clear the reasons for wanting to homeschool. The IEP team is more likely to see the parents' rationale if their reasons are based on the child's needs, not the lack of satisfaction in the school's program. Additionally, showing the team that a parent has done some research and has the means to access the social, behavioral, and academic supports necessary to promote success in the homeschool environment will go a long way in gaining IEP team support.

Members of the IEP team may not feel that the homeschool program is an appropriate program for the child. If this occurs, often

Parent Perspective

Regulations vary by state. In California, "Independent Home Study" is considered an "option" not a "placement." According to the Education Code, each student must have his or her program developed within the context of that student's IEP. Public schools are not obligated to approve a student's transfer to an Independent Home Study program. In some cases, a district may decide (not always for the right reasons) that a student receiving services should remain in the traditional setting.

—Janelle Lewis

informal or formal means of mediation can take place to discuss the child's needs and possible options. If an agreement cannot be reached in informal mediation, more formal steps can be taken, including due process. At this point, a "stay put" for program and services goes into affect, which means that until an agreement is reached or the decision is made by the hearing officer, the program and services remain "as is" based on the last signed IEP.

Private School Placement

When a child (K–12) is parentally placed in a private school, including private or parochial homeschool programs, the child has no individual entitlement to services or funding. The Local Education Agency (LEA) can provide an Individual Service Plan (ISP), which is different from an IEP. The services offered by and through the ISP are based on a funding formula using a proportionate amount of federal funds available to serve parentally placed private school children with disabilities under Federal Code Section 612(a) (10). This figure is based on the number of students with disabilities attending private school at the parent's choice divided by the total number of students with disabilities within the educational agencies' jurisdiction.

The type and level of service offered through a service plan is generally limited to consultation or training to the parents or private school staff or both. The type of consultation is general, often via phone conference, and typically does not exceed five hours per year. The professional providing the consultation can vary depending on the school district, but is often a speech and language specialist.

The LEA is obligated to inform the parent annually of their parental rights and responsibilities and provide educational assessment upon request of the parent; however, these assessments often result in a recommendation to participate in the LEA program. Parents who have already rejected the public school's offering may not want to participate in this assessment process and often seek out their own private assessments, educational consultation, and services through private providers. Depending on your health insurance program, some of the assessments and services that a child with ASD may require can be funded through this resource.

Weigh the Options Carefully

Because services and support such as speech therapy and occupational therapy are often critical for the success of a student with ASD, parents should weigh their options carefully and determine whether they are able to access these services prior to making a final decision about a homeschool program. If these services are not necessary or the family has other means by which to access them (private pay, health insurance, or health services support), then private placement may be the best option. If these services are necessary and the family has no other means of access, they should work hard to secure a public option and establish good communication with the child's IEP team as options are explored.

10 How Should a Family Get Started with Homeschooling?

Step 1: Research

In order to make an informed decision about whether homeschooling is right for a family, research is required. It is important that the parents know both the legal and pragmatic issues related to homeschooling. While homeschooling is now legal in all fifty states and has been since 1993, each state has its own set of regulations.[2] It is vital that parents know the laws that apply in their state. Information can be accessed through each State Department of Education or by contacting the Home School Legal Defense

Parent Perspective

I would recommend speaking with other families and possibly observing their programs in order to see the diverse methods out there.

—Connie Ajay

Association (www.hslda.com). There are also additional regulations that apply for special education services that parents should be informed of. These are covered in more detail in Question 9.

To learn about the practical aspects of homeschooling, it might be best to talk to other families who have made this choice. Additionally, there are many books, Web sites, and online networks that parents can access to find out about homeschooling. Please refer to the resources that are provided throughout this book and in the response to Question 8.

Parents are likely to have many questions initially and as they progress during the first year of the homeschool journey. Identifying local resources for information and support is an important part of the required research. There are many varied philosophies about homeschooling, and they may not all mesh with a parent-teacher's ideas and beliefs. It takes time to find a resource or set of resources that fit the individual teaching style and needs. Although the exact philosophy and style of homeschooling does not need to be solidified before homeschooling begins, a parent-teacher should have several sources of information and support identified to help as they find their way.

Do the Research

- Talk to other families who are doing homeschooling.

- Find out the laws and regulations on homeschooling and special education regulations that apply in your state by contacting your State Department of Education.

- Find local resources for homeschoolers.

- Learn about the various philosophies, structures, and styles of homeschooling.

Step 2: Look at the Pros and Cons

Families should make a decision based on their values and what the family has identified as the pros and cons of homeschooling. This personal choice should be based on the unique situation and needs. Determining the pros and cons for the child and the rest of the family is vital in the decision-making process. Recognizing that there are some downsides to homeschooling and having a realistic perspective is important. Many of the homeschooling advocacy books and resources that are available paint a rosy picture of the homeschooling experience. As a family does the research, we encourage them to talk to other families who have made this choice and ask for their honest feedback about the downsides of homeschooling. This will help develop a clearer picture and allow the family to make a more informed decision.

Many parents we have interviewed indicate that they selected homeschooling because "They had no other choice." They felt as though the public school system was simply not equipped to handle the needs of their child and could not provide a student with ASD with an appropriate educational program. Remember that there are *always* alternatives and ways to meet unique needs. Just because the public school did not get it right the first time does not mean that with some additional training, professional consultation, or support that they cannot do a better job at meeting the child's needs. Sometimes these necessary changes can be made by working with the school district in a collaborative manner. Ask for additional staff to look at the child's needs or bring in new administrators to see if a fresh perspective can offer new directions.

Often, parents feel as if they have attempted to work with the schools, but to no avail. Hiring a professional advocate or bringing in experts to assess the child and the program they are participating in within the public school setting can sometimes help to steer things in a new direction. There may also be private or nonpublic schools in a community that can meet the unique needs of the child with ASD. These options should all be explored. If a parent still feels that homeschooling is the *only* choice, recognize that this forced choice may result in feelings of resentment, frustration, or depression. If this is the situation, the family must work hard to find alternatives or seek professional support and guidance.

Step 3: Develop a Homeschooling Plan

The homeschooling program will be a work-in-progress, and it may take a while to hit a stride. Many feel as though they must have a minute-by-minute schedule and all of the curriculum and resources in place on the first day of the homeschool program. Most experts and families who have embarked on homeschooling advise new homeschoolers to relax and enjoy the first few weeks. According to the Homeschool Association of California, "You won't know what will work best for your family until you've had a chance to spend relaxed time learning, listening, observing, and exploring with your family in your own homeschool setting".[3]

Take some decompression time. Many suggest a period of "decompression," which is time allowed for regrouping and recouping some of the energy that may have been lost during the highly demanding traditional school program. Many children who have been unsuccessful in traditional school programs can benefit from some downtime. This can be time spent simply enjoying daily activities and discovering the things that make the child tick. It can also be time spent assessing the child's natural rhythms. For example, when is he most focused? When does he really need to move or get outside? Having a break from formal lessons can help to undo some of the negative emotional memories that may have resulted from a lack of success in prior learning situations. Once decompression has taken place, ease into a more formal learning program and start with the child's interests and strength areas. This will establish a positive and successful learning experience for both the parent-teacher and the child.

Research a variety of curricula. As a parent begins to plan for and think about the curriculum and what should be taught, they should look for things that work with the child's strengths. Most

Parent Perspective

It is really important for parents who are homeschooling their child with ASD to realize that some days you will really need to work on social, emotional, and behavioral issues more than any academic subject. When I began homeschooling my daughter in sixth grade, we spent the first three months or so working on how to talk to me about very painful emotions without physical outbursts. Social-emotional healing was so much more important than remaining in a traditional school setting. This process "saved" her from herself, and we would not be doing as well today if not for this choice.

—Karen Crum

Table 3.4.   Tried-and-True Curricula and Programs for Students with ASD

Learning Domain	K–3	4th–9th
Reading	Edmark Story Grammar Marker Explode the Code	Comprehension Upgrade Think About! *Learning the R.O.P.E.S. for Improved Executive Function*
Writing	The Writer's Companion Handwriting Without Tears Kidspiration Speedy Keys	The Writer's Companion Inspiration Type to Learn Writing Focus
Math	Touch Math Math Master	Mighty Math

children with ASD learn best using real-world, real-life scenarios where they can learn within a meaningful context. Additionally, visually mediated strategies are often helpful. The computer, using CDs or online classes or programs, also offers many appealing choices to students with ASD. Look for curriculum and learning opportunities that capture these elements. Many of these were discussed in Question 8. Additional curricula that are highly successful with ASD students are indicated in the following example (see Table 3.4).

Prepackaged curricula. Many homeschoolers get started with prepackaged curricula and quickly move on to other things or learn to adapt the curricula to their child's unique style. Some use prepackaged programs longer and find them very effective, and many never use them at all. The Homeschool Association of California suggests that families take time to explore some options before making a commitment or investment in a specific curriculum. Time will help a parent-teacher come to their own wise conclusions about whether to use something that is already laid out, or whether to pick and choose resources as they go along.

Parent
Perspective

Many parents and children feel more comfortable for the first year following a very traditional school routine with textbooks for each subject, with a "chapter a day or week" sort of setup. Utilizing a homeschooling program through a school in your area may be especially helpful in the first year because it will give both the parent and child a clear starting place and guidelines. Also, if the homeschool program offers some type of traditional in-classroom courses, it may make an easier transition so that the child is still in a classroom for at least a few hours each week. It can be difficult for the parent and child at first going from seven hours per day in the classroom to none at all.

—Karen Crum

Parent
Perspective

Ben previously hated going anywhere new and was very anxious about most community settings, so we built frequent opportunities to work on related skills in out-of-home settings into our homeschool days. Taking part in all of these outside activities was not possible when Ben was attending traditional school; he was just too tired and stressed to do anything else when he came home from school. He now accompanies me on errands such as grocery shopping and is involved in decisions and planning that affect our family.

—Janelle Lewis

Plan for extracurricular activities. Identifying and including extracurricular activities is also critical to research and plan for in a fully rounded homeschooling program. It is one of the advantages of homeschooling a child with ASD and also offers many social opportunities that are critical for students with this disability.

Step 4: Make the Move and Complete the Necessary Registration

Depending on the type of program selected, varying registration processes must be completed. We advise families to begin the registration process as soon as possible once a program decision has been made as it may take some time. Parents must also plan for how and when to inform the child's current school about the decision.

Inform the school. There are several factors to consider regarding informing the child's school. The most important factor is whether the family wishes to continue to receive any of the special education services offered through the IEP. If so, then the family will need to go through the IEP process and come to agreement with the IEP team about the change of placement and services that are necessary for the child to benefit from his educational program. As is discussed in Question 9, the services that are available may depend on the type of program selected (public, public charter, or private). Additionally, the other members of the IEP team may not agree with the parents' determination that a homeschooling program is appropriate, which may result in a lengthier process for resolving the issue.

Request a copy of the child's cumulative file. If the family does not anticipate using any of the special education services offered through the public school, the Homeschool Association of California suggests that they simply tell the school that the child will be attending another school and provide them the name of that school. It may not be necessary or beneficial to inform the school that the child is being "homeschooled." Parents can tell school officials whether they are transferring to a public or private school, but they are not obligated to give them any more information than that. The receiving school should write the former school to request the child's cumulative file. If the parent is starting their own private school, then they should promptly write a professional letter to the former school on the school letterhead advising the administrators that the child has been enrolled in (your school name) and request his or her cumulative file.[4]

Step 5: Continue to Access the Needed Support to Prevent Burnout

Parents are encouraged to use the network of support to help them along. One valuable resource and opportunity for networking that many homeschoolers take advantage of are homeschooling conferences or conventions. These provide the parent-teacher with a place to network and talk to other homeschool parents, a place to look at and shop for materials and curriculum, and often workshops to help improve their skills or introduce new strategies or ideas. It can be a great initiation into homeschooling or a way to re-spark the passion and revisit the reasons that homeschooling was chosen to begin with.

Parent Perspective

One of the keys to an easier adjustment to homeschooling is to access many resources during your first year of homeschooling and decide from there which groups seem to suit you and your child's interests and style. You will find you cannot do everything that is offered, but you will settle into routines in time that work for you.

—Karen Crum

4

Questions About Teaching Strategies

11 How Should the Core Deficits of Social Skills and Social Thinking Be Addressed?

For individuals with ASD, reciprocal social interaction requires the same intentional direct instruction that any academic skill requires. Specific goals should be identified, and instructional opportunities to practice social skills must be scheduled throughout the day. The type of strategy selected will depend on the ability of the child. The basic instructional strategies, regardless of the child's skill level, are to present the social instruction in a visual and concrete manner.

Like a pyramid, socialization includes many layers that build upon one another (see Figure 4.1). The first layer is the very foundation of socialization, which is play. The next layer involves reciprocal interactions, including the initiation, maintenance, and termination of a social exchange. The final layer involves the skills necessary for sustained relationships based on shared interests and the ability to take on the perspective of another person. Some of

Feelings of isolation can result at first, unless a plan for socialization has been integrated into the process. Care must be taken to plan for social contact as soon as homeschool begins for both the parent and child.

—Karen Crum

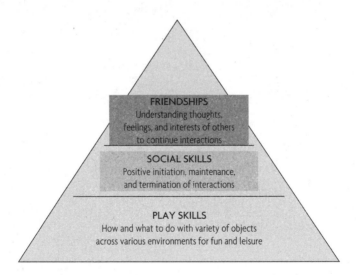

Figure 4.1.   Socialization Pyramid

the skills for socialization include interpreting nonverbal communication, identifying one's own emotions and the emotions of others, expressing empathy, thinking about the wants and needs of another person, and being willing and able to change one's behavior to match the social situation, to name just a few.

Targeted social skills should be taught in a context that is meaningful to the child with ASD and related to real-world situations that

Parent Perspective

I have found that social opportunities have been meaningful since my son has been in homeschool. I am able to place him in opportunities where he is engaging with students who have similar hobbies. For example, he loves drama; therefore, I placed him in the Parks and Recreation drama classes, and he excels in the classes. He shows no embarrassment, and drama is one place where quirkiness is viewed as talent. Therefore, he is viewed as a leader in the class. The students around him don't even know he is on the spectrum, as many of them have some similar quirkiness and similar hobbies.

—Connie Ajay

are experienced on a regular basis. Opportunities for frequent practice and reflection or feedback on skill performance and the outcomes of social behavior are an important part of instruction.

Although parents are the experts on their child and often very intuitive about the approaches to use, it is also helpful to become familiar with the strategies and curriculum demonstrated to be effective for students with ASD. An underlying strategy to ensure success at all ages is to provide social opportunities within a context related to the child's area of interest.

Teaching Play

For the young child who may not yet have a defined topic of interest, it is often best to begin with an object of high interest. Play with objects or "object-focused play" can be a bridge into the child's world. Imitation, joint attention, turn taking, and sharing can easily be taught by following the child's lead and interest in an object.

An excellent instructional video that helps parents learn this important strategy is titled *Embracing Play.*[1]

Moving a child from interacting with objects and adults to actually engaging in reciprocal interactions with peers requires structure and a plan. This can be accomplished by setting up "play dates." These are highly structured, predictable play sessions between a child with ASD and a neurotypical peer. The objective of a play date is shaping active engagement in play and social interaction. By starting out small, with only one other peer, in a highly structured setting and routine, the chances of success are greatly increased. Play dates can be effective for all ages of learners, but are typically used with young children to promote the early development of play and socialization. The following steps will assist a parent in setting up play dates:

Step 1: The parent must identify peers who have already established sound play skills and are considered socially competent. The socially competent play partner becomes a role model for the child with ASD. The play partner must be skillful in social interaction, communication, imagination, and behavior. Finding these play partners may feel like a big task; however, a parent may simply look to the neighborhood, family friends, siblings and their friends, or other community settings in which the family already has social contacts.

Step 2: Disclose the disability to the play-date partners. There are varied opinions about whether the parent should do this. Children are very observant, and even the very young child will recognize differences, especially if the child with ASD struggles with communication or behavior. Author Pamela Wolfberg suggests that the play partner needs some basic information that will assist him or her in understanding how to encourage reciprocal social interaction.[2] This does not require a diagnostic label; however, in some situations recognizing the label is appropriate. Of course, disclosure and the amount of detail provided is always the parent's decision.

Step 3: Initially the play date should be kept short and based on one or two high-interest activities. The setting should be highly structured and predictable to begin with, but can be varied where play dates are held at a community location such as a favorite park, restaurant, or activity center once certain skills are developed. If the play date is held at home, setting up an activity that ends with a product that is reinforcing such as making slice-and-bake cookies is a good idea. By keeping the play date short, neither child is overwhelmed, and the chances of success are greater. Ending with success often leads to both children wanting to meet and play again.

Step 4: As the length of the play date extends, a visual schedule may be used to assist the children in easily moving through activities. The type of visual schedule used will be based on the level of the children involved. Younger children may use a picture schedule, whereas older children may use a written list to organize and sequence the activities they are going to do.

A wonderful resource for learning about play dates is the video called *Passport to Friendship*.[3] This video provides a step-by-step process for setting up and running an effective play date and illustrates how to implement the needed structure and support. The concepts presented and used with young children can be modified for older children. The underlying conditions to ensure a successful play date include planning, preparation, structure, and support.

Teaching Theory of Mind (ToM)

As children with ASD grow and mature, in addition to learning to play with objects and interact with other individuals, they must also be taught to think about the thoughts and feelings of others. The ability to take the perspective of another individual involves "Theory of Mind" (ToM). Most typically developing children have a sense of how their behavior impacts another person's thoughts about them by the age of five or six. As a result of this ToM, they adjust their behavior to have a more positive impact on the playmate. This adjustment is made in order to maintain the social interaction. Children with a good ToM are able to put their own needs and desires aside in order to maintain a positive social interaction with a peer. They are also able to persuade a peer to adopt their ideas about what to play or how to play. Typically children with a strong ToM are highly socially competent individuals. Most of the time, developing children are not explicitly taught ToM, they simply learn it through the natural course of development.

It is well documented that individuals with ASD have a delay in the development of ToM. This delay leads to problems with social interaction as the child with ASD is not able to think about the needs, thoughts, ideas, or feelings of others. Perspective taking must be explicitly taught to children with ASD, as it results in greater social competence. This is a skill that requires a great deal of practice for children with ASD. It can be helpful to follow a predeveloped curriculum for teaching ToM. An example of such a curriculum is *Teaching Children with Autism to Mind-Read* by Howlin, Baron-Cohen, and Hadwin (1999). Another valuable curriculum involving ToM is *Navigating the Social World: A Curriculum for Individuals with Asperger's Syndrome and High Functioning Autism* (2003) by Jeanette McAfee.[4]

When a child has cognitive delays combined with autism, their ability to take the perspective of others is typically severely impaired. For these children, it is generally acknowledged that they will require direct support and modification to sustain social interactions and relationships rather than instruction in perspective taking. This can be accomplished by training the social partner how to interact and support the child. Social skills interventions for more severely disabled individuals should still involve teaching play and leisure skills and appropriate social greetings and manners. The higher-level thinking skills involved in Theory of Mind and perspective taking may be developed much later, well into the adult years, or may remain elusive due to a lack of developmental readiness even into adulthood.

Visually Based Strategies for Teaching Social Thinking

Acknowledging that students with ASD learn best using a visual modality, many authors and practitioners have developed visually mediated strategies for teaching these complex social thinking skills. One of the "tried and true" visual strategies for teaching social understanding is Comic Strip Conversations developed by Carol Gray. In her book *Comic Strip Conversations,* Gray describes how to use simple line drawings and conversation symbols to illustrate "what people say and do, and emphasize what people may be thinking." Using different colors to represent the emotional content of statements, thoughts, and questions provides a way to help children understand complex emotion. This dynamic method can be used to visually problem solve situations and then create an alternate plan for addressing the situations in the future. The comic strip may even become a script for role-playing and practicing social interactions. Comic Strip Conversations give parents and educators a visual and concrete tool to assist children with ASD in understanding complex and abstract social situations.[5]

Students of all ages have also benefited from *White Boards Words and Thoughts* created by Kandis Lighthall and Patricia Schetter.[6] By having a three-dimensional whiteboard in a specific shape that represents things you say (talk board) and things you think (thought board), students can learn to interact with words and ideas in a visual and concrete manner. This physical interaction with the whiteboards allows the student to manipulate his thoughts and words, to think about what to say, or to consider how certain words or actions might impact another person's feelings. The boards are a valuable tool in role-playing and practicing the use of social scripts. For example, you can role-play how the child might ask someone to play. The student writes his words on the talk board after thinking about what to say and how to say it. He then practices the response. The teacher or peer fills in their thought board indicating how they feel about the way the student asked them to play. The student can change his words or actions based on the effect it had on the partner. This dynamic interaction allows the student to see how his behavior affects the thoughts of another person, providing immediate and concrete feedback.

Younger children can practice social requests and comments using the whiteboards. The boards can be incorporated into typical games or drama. Older children may find the boards a fun way to communicate nonverbally. Parents can make the boards or obtain the boards and instruction booklet through www.autismandbehavior.com.

Another effective strategy developed by Carol Gray is Social Stories. The book *Social Stories 10.0* defines the criteria and guidelines for writing this specific type of story. A social story has a defined style and format that "describes a situation, skill, or concept in terms of relevant social cues, perspectives, and common responses" (p. 2). Social Stories are based on the child's personal experiences and his or her responses to situations. A social story should have a reassuring nature and strive to teach social understanding as opposed to rote compliance to social rules. The first consideration in writing a social story is to identify a story topic that applauds achievements. Carol Gray suggests that 50 percent of all stories should be positive in nature (p. 3). Eventually the stories can also describe and clarify difficult situations and help individuals learn to understand the perspective of others in the situation. Social Stories, when written and used correctly, can support social learning and behavioral changes. To learn more about writing Social Stories refer to *Social Stories 10.0* and *The New Social Story Book,* or investigate The Gray Center for Social Learning and

Understanding, a nonprofit organization serving people with ASD and people who work on behalf of individuals with ASD.[7]

Michelle Garcia-Winner, a speech and language pathologist, author, and lecturer, has offered many strategies in her books to assist individuals with ASD and other social cognitive impairments develop an understanding of social situations. Her focus is to help learners develop an understanding of the perspectives of others. In her book *Inside Out: What Makes a Person with Social Cognitive Deficits Tick?* (2000), Michelle lays the foundation to help parents and educators understand the underlying difficulties a person with ASD experiences. Garcia-Winner has published many additional resources that offer guidance as well as worksheets, lessons, and goals to assist anyone trying to teach social understanding. Parents may find such strategies as "Friendship File" in Garcia-Winner's curriculum workbook particularly helpful. A video lecture and demonstrations of her interventions are also available, which offer parents a hands-on illustration of how to work with

Parent Perspective

We use the *Navigating the Social World* curriculum by Jeanette McAfee in the freshman Personal Growth class at the charter homeschool my son attends. We have discussions about how other people feel. We use social comic strips (Carol Gray) and social autopsies (Michelle Garcia-Winner) to review blunders. I consider his lab times at the homeschool facility to be social practice sessions.

—Ann Coe

Parent Perspective

The beauty of homeschool is that a social thinking curriculum can be one of the primary topics of the child's course of study. If parents are resourceful and creative, groups or activities can be developed for practical opportunities to practice social thinking and interaction. A friend or acquaintance can even be hired as a social assistant for the child with ASD. Parents may wish to seek out the support of a specialist in social skills and have them help with this part of the education, just as some parents seek help in teaching academic subjects.

—Karen Crum

students on the skills for social understanding. To acquire information about Michelle Garcia-Winner, visit her Web site at www .socialthinking.com.[8]

Given that socialization is one of the core deficits for students with ASD, it must be a major focus whether the child is homeschooled or attending a traditional school program. Social events happen everywhere, and incidental teaching (teaching as a naturally occurring event happens) is one strategy that should be used. However, it is the belief of many autism experts that to achieve a fundamental understanding of social dynamics, direct instruction incorporating visually mediated strategies is necessary. Parents who homeschool their child are strongly encouraged to consider incorporating any or all of the visual methods discussed in this section into their daily instruction.

12 How Can Social Opportunities Be Incorporated into the Homeschooler's Day?

How to incorporate social opportunities during homeschool is a common concern of parents and educators. Given that one of the core deficits of ASD is impairment in reciprocal social interaction, this question is even more significant when considering homeschool for a child with ASD. The concern that there will be *no social opportunities* is often the major obstacle voiced against homeschooling a child with ASD by professionals, family members, and friends of families who want to homeschool their child with ASD.

Parent Perspective

It is a common misconception that homeschoolers are socially isolated. Children with ASD tend to be more socially isolated (sometimes self-imposed) at traditional school than in the homeschool setting. Home-schoolers may be involved in all sorts of clubs, groups, and activities that offer quality social experiences within their realm of interest. My son has found fellow homeschoolers with whom he shares many interests, and they tend to be far less judgmental than the kids were at his traditional school. He is also more comfortable interacting across age ranges, as he is in social contact with many more adults and older children now that he is homeschooled.

—Janelle Lewis

Social Advantages in Homeschool

Rather than seeing socialization as a reason not to homeschool, many families with children of varied ability levels consider socialization as the "ultimate reason" for homeschooling their child. Some students with ASD have described traditional school as "torturous, confusing, scary, and frustrating." This is typically due to a combination of academic and social demands that the student with ASD is confronted with on a traditional school campus. Students who have fewer skills often comment on the school setting through their "unconventional behavior." Asking some children with ASD to happily attend school compares with asking an individual who has difficulty with mobility to participate in highly physical activities all day at school. These physical demands might be too much for the individual with mobility issues and could cause great anxiety, stress, and an inability to function successfully. Yet students with ASD who have a core deficit in reciprocal social interaction are expected to perform daily in an appropriate social manner from the minute they step on the campus until they leave at the end of the day. They are expected to use appropriate greetings, ask for help, work cooperatively in groups, understand nonverbal communication, play with others, participate in games, and understand the hidden social curriculum that is never directly taught to anyone. For students with ASD who have average to above-average intelligence and achievement, social support is infrequently considered necessary by school personnel. Their academic success masks the need for social interventions. For students with ASD who have cognitive delays, the social support is frequently provided by school personnel; however, the whole environment may be too stimulating for them to benefit from the supports and efforts to teach social skills.

The literature on homeschooling all children, including children with ASD, refutes the concerns that there are limited social opportunities. What is typically reported is that there are so many social opportunities that the options must be prioritized. The beauty of social opportunities in a homeschool situation is that they can be more customized to the individual child's needs and interests. Parents must remember that the type and intensity of appropriate social experiences for a child with ASD may vary greatly from that of neurotypical peers. Social growth may be measured very differently for a child with ASD. A traditional school campus may present far too many social situations for a child with ASD to cope with and little time for small-group or highly structured social encounters.

Same-aged, typically developing peers may not be the optimal social skills teachers. Sherri Linsenbach, founder and president of homeschoolfun.com, states the following regarding social skills and peers: "Peers can't take the place of ones family . . . A child's peers usually aren't any more mature than the child himself, and they can't always display good judgment or proper decision making skills."[9] Parents honor the social differences far easier than peers do in the traditional school setting. In a homeschooling situation, a parent and child can develop the opportunities that do not overwhelm the child, helping him become more eager to participate in a variety of social opportunities.

Socialization Within Family Routines

The first place to think about social opportunities is in the home within events that occur naturally. Families may try to plan mealtimes where everyone can be together. This is a perfect time to talk about things that are of interest to each person. The conversation may require more structure and possibly some visually mediated strategies to help initially with asking questions or making comments. An example of a visually mediated strategy involves placing either a question card or comment card in front of each family member. Each person takes a turn either asking another person a question or making a comment based on what their card says. Parents and siblings model this procedure and encourage the child with ASD to take his turn.

Other social opportunities that occur within the family include birthday parties, visits from relatives or friends, play dates, sleepovers, and family chores such as raking leaves, gardening, or preparing meals. When two or more people are together, it is a social situation and a natural opportunity to teach social interaction, empathy, and perspective taking of others. The Web site Go Ask Anyone.com (www.goaskanyone.com) offers parents and educators a creative series of conversation cards that can be used in many different ways. The cards help to get conversations going on

Parent Perspective

Homeschooling can be a great arena for addressing social cognition deficits. We use some mapped-out social skills lessons, but, more naturally, we are interacting and conversing all day—much more so than when he was at school. We talk about emotions, feelings, intentions, and perceptions throughout literature and history lessons. Perspective taking has come much more into focus with my son as we have tied it into the stories that we are reading. We role-play quite a bit, with ourselves and with action figures and stuffed animals. My son also attends a social skills therapy group and has done social skills drama groups. Addressing social thinking in lesson formats, naturally, and in small-group settings all in relatively stress-free environments is helping tremendously with his self-confidence in other social settings.

—Janelle Lewis

topics that are appropriate to a variety of individuals and can be used in various environments and events. These conversation cards can also be used to build literary and writing skills.

Social Opportunities Outside the Home

Moving outside the home may access a variety of extracurricular activities offered through community, school, or homeschool groups that are age appropriate and of interest to homeschoolers. Many families already have a network of social activities that they participate in on a regular basis. These may be through their church, parks and recreation departments, clubs, or organizations. Typically within each of these options there are activities for different age groups. If a family has concerns that certain accommodations might be required, they can have a conversation with the leader of the program to explain the social goals and challenges that are being worked on. Finding the correct "social fit" often requires some disclosure about the child, the disability, and the unique needs in order to ensure success.

For some individuals, performing arts are an excellent resource. Drama involves many skills that may benefit a child with ASD, such as following a script, opportunities for imitation, and practice expressing and understanding nonverbal and verbal communication. Many parents and professionals have recognized the social benefits of drama classes. Author Amelia Davies has written a curriculum titled *Teaching Asperger's Students Social Skills Through Acting: All Their World's a Stage!* (2004). This resource provides an overview for teaching social skills through drama with suggested activities that can be implemented across age groups.[10]

Other individuals with ASD may enjoy dance or music classes. Individual sports such as karate, swimming, golf, and tennis allow the child to learn a skill individually while being part of a group. Sports are typically only successful if the child has an interest and does not feel physically awkward about his movement. Sports or health clubs also provide a great family opportunity to make fitness a group activity and help to develop lifelong expectations for good health. Scouting can provide small-group social opportunities with chances to follow personal interest when earning badges. Individuals with interests in animals might try 4-H. There are many opportunities in 4-H to work alone or with the group.

Community service or volunteer work is an avenue to provide social opportunities and develop leadership skills. A museum, zoo, or library could be a location where an individual can engage with others who share a common interest. Performing the duties of a "student guide" provides an opportunity to talk about personal interests and receive positive acknowledgment for this. The student guides are often paired with an adult leader who can assist by coaching the student in leadership and social relationships. Parents have reported that volunteer positions are often very motivating to children with ASD. To maintain these positions, good planning and ongoing communication between the parents and staff at the volunteer site are required.

Children who are involved in homeschool may actually have more time to devote to social skills development than children in traditional school settings. This additional time is very important to children with ASD. Because these social opportunities are community-based, the children have an opportunity to interact with various age groups in a variety of situations often with a common interest that is shared by all participants. Social situations become a choice based on an interest instead of a requirement based on a grade level and school campus schedule.

It must be recognized that social skills teaching is a lifelong pursuit for individuals with ASD. There is no one curriculum that will address all that is needed. These skills must be taught, practiced, and reinforced over a lifetime. As stated by Temple Grandin, "It's not a topic that starts at a certain age and then stops . . . Social

Parent Perspective

I have personally found that the areas of social thinking can be addressed more thoroughly through homeschooling because I can address the issues as they happen. Furthermore, my son has the time to be able to fully explore social dilemmas without having to worry about missing a lesson or having to do homework before addressing the social component. The traditional school setting does not allow adequate time to teach the social skills that students with ASD often struggle with due to time constraints. Furthermore, the system is not set up to teach these lessons because the typical student does not often require social skills training. As a result, the schools are oftentimes not equipped to teach the social skills curriculum that is a necessity for students with ASD.

—Connie Ajay

awareness can't be neatly covered by a single textbook so that when you get to the last page, you can close the book and be educated. This is a book that has no last page."[11]

13 | How Should the Core Deficits in Organizational Skills and Thinking Be Addressed?

While anyone who works with children on the Autism Spectrum is familiar with their challenges in organizational skills and thinking, most do not know that there is an underlying neurological basis for these challenges. To answer this question, we will begin by presenting information about the neurological basis of this deficit. Following this overview, practical strategies to assist with organizational skills and thinking will be provided.

The Deficit in Executive Functioning (EF)

It is becoming broadly recognized that deficits in organizational skills and organizational thinking are central deficits for individuals with ASD that impact their functioning across many life domains. The deficits are referred to in the neuropsychology literature as impaired executive functioning (EF). Executive functions are the cognitive processes thought to be responsible for many of our problem-solving skills and abilities. They are the planning processes that we automatically use at the beginning of a task and when dealing with novel situations. The region of the brain thought to be central in executive functioning is the prefrontal cortex. Many recent studies using neuroimaging indicate that individuals with ASD have impaired prefrontal functioning, which helps to explain the decrease in executive functioning seen across the autism spectrum.

Executive Functions That Are Impaired in ASD

Ozonoff and Schetter reported that individuals with ASD have certain components of executive functioning that are impaired, including organization and planning skills, self-monitoring, and goal-directed behavior. People with ASD also demonstrate difficulty with working memory and have deficits in flexibility at a conceptual level, including shifting from one category or topic to another and at an attentional level such as disengaging and moving their attention from one place to another.[12]

As a result of these cognitive deficits, we see characteristic patterns of behavior and problems in the development of certain skills and abilities. Executive impairments can cause a host of difficulties that may go unrecognized or be misinterpreted by those who do not understand this aspect of the disability. A singular focus on special topics, difficulty transitioning between activities or relinquishing favored objects, resistance to change, repetitive language and motor behavior, and tendency to perseverate on ways of doing things are all signs of executive dysfunction.[13]

The skill deficits associated with these impairments include failure to develop an understanding of cause and effect related to their own behavior; an inability to predict outcomes or think about consequences; poor organizational skills related to personal space; and problems with planning for upcoming events, including activities, conversations, or written communications. When one looks closely at many of the learning problems that children with ASD have across the curriculum, it becomes clear that many academic challenges tie directly to the impairments in executive functioning. For example, reading comprehension is often very difficult for students with ASD because it requires them to predict and make guesses and assumptions about the behavior, thoughts, and feelings of others. These skills require the student to keep facts organized and recall them, integrate them, and plan for the potential outcome of events—all requiring executive functioning.

Impacts of Executive Dysfunction on Life Skills

We commonly see EF issues carry over into life skills and adaptive functioning. Individuals with impaired executive functioning often have poor time management and require a high level of support to complete life-skill routines in a timely manner. The organizational deficits often result in poor work performance and social problems as the person fails to think about how his behavior will affect or be interpreted by others. EF impairments affect those with higher-functioning autism as well as those who have cognitive impairments. In individuals with fewer cognitive skills, organizational deficits are often manifest in problems with transitioning from one activity to another or problems with completing even well-practiced routines.

Interventions for Executive Dysfunction

Executive dysfunction must be addressed as a priority goal of intervention due to the broad-sweeping implications of these deficits. There are two equally important components to intervention for executive dysfunction:

1. Teaching the student to work around the deficits through accommodations, modifications, and compensatory strategies

2. Directly training weak or missing skills using targeted interventions that capture the learning strengths of individuals with ASD

There are many things that a parent-teacher can do to support the EF needs of the homeschooled student with ASD. In fact, this is an area that can and should be interwoven into all other activities throughout the day. The ability to weave in the EF interventions is a major advantage to homeschooling a child with ASD. By making this a core feature of all lessons, the parent-teacher can provide the much-needed practice within meaningful, real-world contexts that will promote growth and development.

Create systems of physical organization. Setting up a highly visually organized physical environment where materials are stored neatly with labels and containers is essential in accommodating the organizational skill deficits of the child. The systems that are initially set up for the child will eventually serve as a springboard into more organized thinking. Once the physical organization systems are set up, the child must be taught about and reinforced for using them. This should be made part of the daily routine. For example, let's say the child's closet is organized with containers and labels on each drawer and on each shelf. The child should be taught to use the system to put away the clothes from the laundry and to gather all of the items needed for dressing each day. A checklist can also be added to the routine to help organize the steps and promote independence with task initiation and completion. The parent's cues should help the child reference the checklist and physical organizational system as part of the daily routine. The strategy changes from giving direct verbal prompts, such as "Now get your socks," to providing indirect prompts that cue the child to use the system provided, such as "What comes next? Look at your list." Toys, dishes, art supplies, and school supplies can all be set up in the same way.

These systems can be used whether the child is higher functioning or has fewer cognitive skills. For younger or more severely impacted children, the organizational systems should be made using photos or concrete visual representations such as an actual object. For more advanced learners, the systems can be written or typed. A label maker is a good investment if you plan to implement visual structure for a reader as described above.

Once the child has had practice using many of these systems, the next step is to work with the child on developing his own systems for physical organization. Perhaps he develops a system for keeping his movies organized. Perhaps he develops an organizational system for his grooming supplies and a morning routine checklist. The important thing is that he becomes part of the process and learns how to plan and manage space and materials.

Create systems of time organization. As described above, the parent-teacher should start by modeling the use of a system for the child. In the case of time management, this involves developing a daily schedule or list of things to do. Keeping a monthly planner of appointments and modeling how to record things is also essential. After the child has seen the parent-teacher using the system, the next step is to involve him in the process. This involvement can take place on a daily basis by sitting down to create a daily list or schedule of things to do. As the parent-teacher and child develop these lists, it creates a wonderful opportunity to talk about priorities, estimate how long things will take, plan efficiently for outings using the map, and so on. Eventually, the development and management

Parent Perspective

What is now working well for us in terms of planning our days is presenting Ben with the tasks that need to be accomplished. Ben creates a whiteboard or paper checklist, which is prioritized and checked off or erased as we do what needs to get done. He also creates a list of things that he really "wants" to do, if what he "needs" to do gets done. The "want to do" list may include things like playing a card game, playing with the dogs, and building with LEGOs. Sometimes activities from the "want to do" list are interspersed with the "need to do" list, depending upon how frequently we need to reinforce what is getting accomplished. When he creates his own schedule, he looks at it much more favorably, and he is more motivated to get things done than if I had presented him with my list.

—Janelle Lewis

of the schedule or "to do" list is turned over to the child, with only minimal support and assistance from the parent-teacher as needed.

For younger children or those with fewer cognitive skills, a visual schedule using photos that depict the order of upcoming events can serve the same function. In the beginning, the parent makes and operates the system, showing the child the process. Eventually, the child should be the one manipulating and even setting up the picture schedule. When using this type of picture schedule, it is important to have a way to indicate when the activities are finished. The child can learn to simply remove the picture and put it into a finished folder or cross it off using a pen.

Parent Perspective

As part of his program, Bobby keeps a calendar in which he organizes his day, including outside appointments and social appointments. I have been able to fully implement an organizational strategy with my son since I oversee his instruction and know exactly where he is lacking and where his strengths are. This has enabled him to be more independent and less prompt-dependent on me or an aide.

—Connie Ajay

Create systems of cognitive organization. How do you make the leap from physical organization and time management to having more organized thoughts? This is where it appears to get more complicated, but really, the same process described above is employed. First, the parent-teacher will model good organizational thinking for the child, then increasingly involve the child in the process, and eventually turn it over to him with only minimal support. The real trick in helping with organizational thinking is to *stop talking and start showing the child visually* how to think through situations.

For those younger children or children with more severe cognitive delays, the goal of using the systems as described above may be appropriate. It may take these children longer to reach the cognitive organization level of intervention, and for some, this level may not be appropriate even into the teenage years.

The following graphic organizers are components of the comprehensive curriculum for teaching organizational thinking called *Learning the R.O.P.E.S. for Improved Executive Functioning.*[14] These organizers provide a way of helping the child with ASD to think through simple and complex organizational processes. By modeling the use of these tools, involving the child in using them to evaluate or analyze situations and activities, and then eventually allowing him to use these tools to think through complex tasks, you will be teaching him to organize his thoughts. These *thinking tools* (as many of our students have begun to call them) may eventually be an internal part of the way the child learns to problem solve and think about events. In essence, by using these tools the child is learning to be a more organized thinker.

Thinking Tool #1: The Venn Diagram

In order to plan for and know how to deal with novel situations, we must teach our kids to draw on existing knowledge. They must also learn to see how events, tasks, and even people are similar to each other (see Figures 4.2 through 4.5). These skills are critical for planning as well as understanding social relationships. The following examples illustrate how this simple graphic organizer can be used to help children with ASD organize needed information across a variety of life activities and academic tasks.

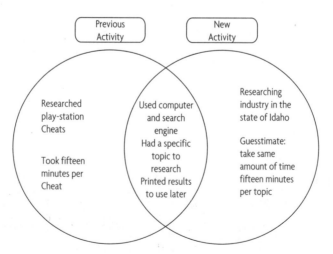

Figure 4.2. Comparing Old and New Activities

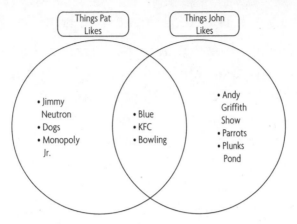

Figure 4.3.   Comparing People's Likes and Interests

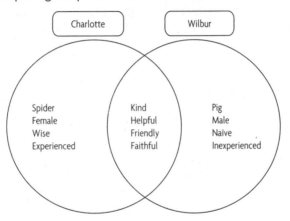

Figure 4.4.   Comparing Characters from Literature

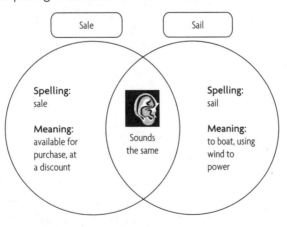

Figure 4.5.   Comparing Homophones

Thinking Tool #2: The Sequential Thinking Tool

A critical thinking error that must be corrected through repeated practice using this sequential thinking tool is to understand the relationship between action and outcome. People who lack good executive functioning often believe that situations occur that cause them to act a certain way and outcomes occur that are out of their control. They fail to see the relationship between situation, action, and outcome. Not understanding this relationship results in feelings of frustration and helplessness and often leads to many mistakes in judgment and planning.

To teach this critical organizational skill, start with the positive (see Figure 4.6). On a daily basis, discuss with the child a situation that occurred that had a desirable outcome. Fill in the graphic organizer illustrating what action(s) he did that contributed to the desired outcome. As the child becomes more independent with the use of this thinking tool, begin to use it for choice making (Figure 4.7), prediction and inference (Figures 4.8), perspective taking (Figure 4.9), and organizing (Figure 4.10), as illustrated in the figures.

Thinking Tool #3: The Cluster Organizer

This thinking tool is used to teach the process of breaking tasks down into chunks, steps, or manageable pieces. Many people who struggle with executive functioning are not able to take a complex

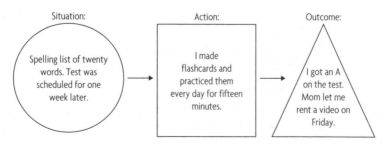

Figure 4.6.   Thinking Tool Evaluating Positive Outcomes

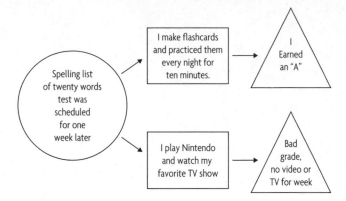

Figure 4.7.   Thinking Tool for Choice Making

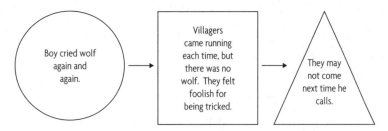

Figure 4.8.   Thinking Tool for Prediction and Inference in Literature

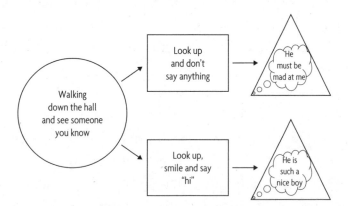

Figure 4.9.   Thinking Tool for Perspective Taking

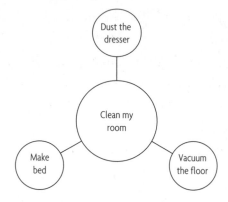

Figure 4.10.   Cluster Organizer for Breaking Down Tasks

task that has multiple steps and break it down into a logical sequence or step-by-step process. They get lost in the process or procrastinate because they legitimately do not know where to begin. Chunking can be taught and illustrated using a cluster organizer. Once a task is broken into pieces, the chunks can be put into a logical sequence and checklist to aide in task completion (refer to Figure 4.13).

To teach chunking, the parent-teacher should begin with simple everyday tasks or routines. Have the child detail the steps of how to complete the task. Fill in the organizer as he describes the pieces (Figure 4.10). The chunks do not need to be in a logical order at this point; the goal is simply for the child to identify all the pieces. Once the chunks are broken out, the next step is putting them in order. As the parent-teacher and child put the steps in order, they should talk about why they belong in a specific order. The parent-teacher should ask questions that will guide the child's thought process. For example, "Why might we want to make the bed before we vacuum?" Guide the child to the correct conclusion. In this example, "It will make it easier because the covers will be out of the way." This problem-solving process can be illustrated using the sequential thinking tool described above (showing the child the outcome if you vacuum with covers still on the floor versus vacuuming when the covers are out of the way).

Identifying the needed materials to complete the task is also a critical organizational component. This can be illustrated using a different color or shape on the cluster organizer (see Figure 4.11). Because of problems with paying attention, an issue common in children with ASD, we advise teaching the child to gather all of the necessary materials for task completion prior to starting the task itself. Often when the child leaves the area to get an item, he becomes distracted or strays off task. Transferring the information from the cluster organizer to a materials checklist and then working on gathering the materials using the checklist to stay focused is a very important skill to work on. This process should be completed across multiple real-world skills until the child is able to complete a cluster for chunking independently.

The cluster organizer can be applied in the same way to academic tasks as illustrated in Figure 4.12. Breaking down complex assignments or research papers, book reports, or even taking notes from reading or a field trip (refer to Figure 4.14) can all be accomplished using the cluster organizer. Once the task is broke down, a checklist

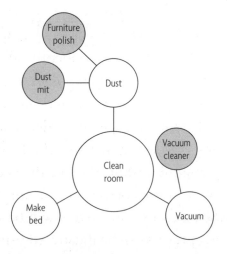

Figure 4.11.   Cluster Organizer for Identification of Materials

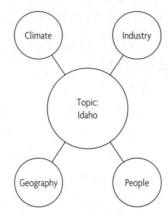

Figure 4.12.   Cluster Organizer for Academic Task

✓	**Researching Idaho**
	Identify subtopics
	Go to library
	Find two to three books with subtopic info
	Photocopy pages with subtopic info
	Go online
	Download two to three articles on each topic
	Highlight important info from articles and photocopied chapters
Reviewed	

Figure 4.13.   Research Project Checklist

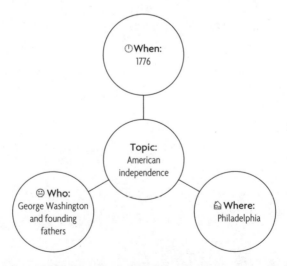

Figure 4.14.   Cluster Organizer for Note Taking

can help to support the child through task completion (refer to Figure 4.13).

Teaching Independence

Remember that all efficacious treatments for children with ASD involve parents in some role.[15] Because the parent has chosen to homeschool their child, they are taking the lead in ensuring the child's educational success. Teaching the organizational skills described in this section are vital, not only for academic success but for success in life. Infusing these skills in daily teaching practices as often as possible will not only help the child become a better student but will help him become a more independent person.

14 How Can Interests Be Incorporated into Instruction?

One of the many advantages of homeschooling that is reported by parents of children with and without ASD is the ability to infuse

Parent Perspective

Ben is much more organized now. We have had the luxury of taking our time to learn and implement executive functioning skills that he was lacking. He helps create our daily and weekly schedule, refers to his planner, organizes his binder and school supplies, and keeps track of time for us. Organizational skills and thinking can be addressed throughout the day as you are homeschooling.

—Janelle Lewis

the child's interests into instruction. Infusing the child's interests is critical to developing and establishing motivation for learning.

There are many individuals with an ASD, including Temple Grandin, Stephen Shore, Daniel Tammet, Donna Williams, and Liane Holliday Willey, who have shared "the world of autism" through their books. Through their life stories, they have described how their special interests have motivated them to do their very best work or develop a career path that has been personally rewarding and provided a positive contribution to society. Their comments indicate that when their teachers allowed them to pursue their topics of interest, they were more motivated to engage in academic work. In fact, their final projects were often much longer and more detailed than the other students in the class.

Parent Perspective

One of the beauties of homeschooling is that instruction is individualized, and the child's interests can drive or be incorporated into what is being learned. It is highly motivational for the child to be able to learn new skills within the framework of what he or she enjoys. Areas of interest can be woven throughout the curriculum, even if you are following prescribed grade-level standards. Reading and writing objectives can be met through child-selected topics. Field trips and art projects can revolve around interests. If science is a passion, much of the curriculum can be science-based. A child's favorite toys can be used in math and creative writing. Whatever the interest is, it can be incorporated into home instruction much easier than in the traditional classroom setting.

—Janelle Lewis

Parents usually know the interests of their child better than anyone. This knowledge is the key to selecting materials that are intrinsically motivating. If a child is interested in animals, a parent may use this topic to select literature for the child to read. Language arts activities such as learning parts of speech, editing, spelling, and so forth, may follow the animal theme. Math can also be based on animal habits. The child may count the number of animals in a herd, flock, or pod and then do a comparison graph that requires calculation. Any basic mathematics function can be applied to the topic of animals. The curriculum area of history can also focus on animals and their role and relationship to man. The focus could also take the student into the community to explore vocations with animals, how animals help people, the health and care of animals, and so on. These interest-focused learning activities may open the door to career development. Temple Grandin is a perfect example of this. Her interest in animals has become her life's work and, as she says, her life. Through her interest in animals she has influenced the handling of livestock at an international level.[16]

A recently published book entitled *Just Give Him the Whale!* provides educators with twenty ways to use an individual's interests

Parent Perspective

My son has written about Pokemon, computer games, volcanoes, Avian flu, sudden oak death, Harry Potter, and historical figures. I have had to change the topic a couple of times when he sat in front of the computer for hours without getting anything written.

—Ann Coe

to motivate learning.[17] Although this book was developed to help educators become more creative in using a student's interests to motivate learning, it may also be helpful to parents who are taking on the role of teacher.

Another resource that provides ways of incorporating the child's interests is *Power Cards: Using Special Interests to Motivate Children and Youth with Asperger Syndrome and Autism.* The author describes the "Power Card Strategy as a visual aid developed by educators and parents to assist students with Asperger Syndrome and autism in making sense of social situations, routines, the meaning of language, and the hidden curriculum that surrounds us wherever we go." The Power Card Strategy is easy to incorporate into a student's daily life. The student is given a short scenario on a single sheet of paper or a card that can be as small as a business card which is about his or her special interest or person. By using the student's personal interest, there is a greater likelihood that the student will attend to the message and follow the directions or guidance offered in the scenario.[18]

Table 4.1 provides a sample of how one might use the Power Card strategy for a student who likes animals and has difficulty with social greetings.

Power Cards may be customized for any age group. This strategy works best with children who have some degree of responsiveness to pictures or written words. Pictures can be used with children who do not read; however, the author states that the strategy is not for everyone and the use of the strategy should be determined on an individual basis.

Another way to incorporate the interest is to allow time to engage in the interest area following the completion of a less-desired activity. Making this contingent with access to the activity

Table 4.1.   Power Card Example

How Does a Dog Say Hello?	Just Like a Dog, I Can Say Hello Too!
A dog may walk up to a person and look at them.	I will try to remember to walk up to a person and look at them.
The dog wags his tail and sometimes puts up his paw.	I can either wave my hand or shake hands with the person and say hello.
The dog is saying hello in his own way.	
People usually feel happy when a dog says hello with a wagging tail or paw.	People usually are happy when I wave or shake hands to say hello.
	I may feel happy too when I see their smile after I say hello.

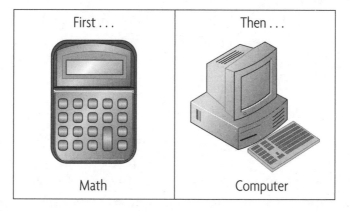

Figure 4.15.   Visual Motivation Strategy

or topic throughout the day can help the student to complete less-desired "work" because he knows he will have access to his preferred activity or interest following the completion of the work. A visual schedule or checklist that indicates when access will occur can be very helpful in setting up this kind of condition, as seen in Figure 4.15. This technique can also be referred to as "sandwiching."

> ## Parent Perspective
>
> Last summer my son worked five hours a week on Algebra. The deal was that if he did that he would be *allowed to take Chemistry* in the fall. As his facilitator said, "That's not a deal that a lot of kids would go for."
>
> —Ann Coe

When a parent knows and uses the interests of their child, they may be able to motivate a child to accomplish even the most challenging of tasks.

15 | How Should the Daily Schedule Be Designed?

Setting up a manageable schedule, for the parent-teacher and the child, and determining the activities that will promote the highest level of engagement in learning with the least amount of stress and anxiety are the primary objectives. There is no *one way* to accomplish this. Each child is unique, and the daily schedule should reflect this. In fact, the annual school calendar will be individualized to meet the child's and family's needs. Some families opt for a traditional school year, running September through May. Others run a year-round program, with family vacations and trips offering a valuable source for experiential instruction.

Let's look at the daily schedules of a few homeschool students to get some ideas.

An Average Instructional Day For Justin

After I take my older son to school, Justin is to be out of bed and finished with his morning routine (washed face, breakfast, and brushed teeth). We begin with Math, English, and Reading and then take a break. We resume with Social Studies and Science and then have lunch. After lunch, he is ready for P.E. There are weeks when we have to work on Saturdays because something may have come up during the week. I try to keep it as routine as possible. He needs the consistency.

—Michelle King

Katie's Schedule

There are changes from year to year as we incorporate one or two public or private school classes into her schedule, and we work around these classes. Also there are different priorities for each year. This year, the priorities are having Katie take care of her school work and home chores/responsibilities more independently.

Currently, this is our schedule:

8 or 9 A.M: Katie wakes up (she is not a morning person). Shower, breakfast, read the newspaper, and discuss it if interesting.

9 or 10–11:30: Katie will usually work independently on two subjects in the morning and finish the third in the afternoon. The subjects are: Language Arts (grammar, vocabulary, reading, writing) and World History or Earth Science (reading and answering questions out of the books). I will help if Katie asks questions, or sometimes we will read together if it is a particularly difficult or abstract assignment. As a sophomore in high school, she can now plan and assign much of her own work in order to keep on track for finishing a subject.

(*Continued*)

Tuesday mornings from 10:00–12:00: Art class at Shasta Secondary Homeschool

Thursday mornings from 9:00–10:00: Horseback riding lessons

11:30: Leave for High School

11:55–12:35 P.M.: Lunch with friends at High School

12:40–1:30: Algebra 1B at High School

2:00: Return home, finish school work left over from morning, occasionally run an errand or visit the library

3:00–4:00: Watch favorite TV show, sometimes on treadmill for exercise (P.E.)

4:00–6:00: May do chores, walk/jog with the dog (P.E.), or play on the computer, or a combination of these three, depending on the day

6:00–9:00: Dinner, family time, Church Youth Group on Tuesday

9:00: Complete bedtime routine, read in bed, bedtime

Katie also attends a social group and participates in Challenger baseball on Saturdays, depending on the time of the year. Over the years, she has played on after-school soccer teams, taken karate lessons and tennis lessons, and attended drama classes. She attends a class to prepare for an upcoming Bible Bowl competition with her church youth group. We may soon add a volunteer experience to the weekly schedule to practice job skills. Katie has worked as a docent at a local museum, worked for a pet adoption clinic, and helped in Children's Worship at church. I consider all of these to be a very valuable part of her "life" curriculum.

—Karen Crum

Ben's School Schedule and Activities

Ben and I have evolved in our approach to the instructional day, and, although we have a schedule, there is great variety in our daily routine within that schedule. Some of the reasons that we chose to homeschool include providing Ben with many more opportunities for community outings, developing better functional life skills, and experiencing quality social interactions.

At-home structured school time usually begins early (by 7:30 A.M.) and ends by noon. Ben performs and stays focused much better if we do our more-structured lessons earlier in the day. We start with Morning Warm-Ups, which review previously learned concepts. Usually, we do Math after Warm-Ups, followed by a break (Ben loves to have "recess" in the backyard with his dogs). English–Language Arts, Social Studies, and Science are quite often integrated thematically and tied in with literature, so it is hard to say what typically comes after that. We fit home P.E. activities (such as jogging, shooting hoops in the yard, long walks, exercising with Nintendo Wii, dancing, and playing catch) in throughout the school day; the physical activity often serves to refocus him. A visual Time Timer is used as an aide to help stay on task, if appropriate, during certain activities.

Because of the possibility that Ben might return to the traditional classroom setting for sixth grade, we have worked a lot of school-type organizational skills into our routine. Ben has a subject-divided binder that we use as appropriate, and if we are taking our school day on the road, he brings a backpack and that binder. We do get a lot of practice, review, and maintenance of skills and knowledge accomplished while driving in the car.

Some days are far more structured than others, depending on what our objectives are. I have purposely built in the flexibility factor so that he can learn to better adapt to change. We have had days where we never even get out of our pajamas and get so into a topic or activity that much

(Continued)

of what we have planned gets carried over to the next day. Some days we really need to work on social, emotional, and behavioral issues more than academics, so that is what we do. Some days we are never even at home during the "homeschool" day. Homeschooling affords us the opportunity to do what feels right on that day, at that time—to individualize our days, hours, minutes according to whatever factors may be influencing focus, behavior, and needs, yet to still practice the academic, organizational, functional, and social/emotional skills needed for future success in the traditional school and work setting, if that is the route Ben takes.

—Janelle Lewis

Bobby's Schedule

We start school at 9:00 A.M., usually with Algebra and pre-Algebra since he is fresher and more focused in the morning. We work until approximately 10:30 when we take a break and walk the dog. Next, we get ready for karate class, which commences at 11:15 until 12:00. Upon returning home we eat lunch and then start school again from 1:00 until 3:00. A couple of days per week he attends RSP classes, speech and occupational therapy classes at the Charter School. At 3:00 he goes on the computer to do the curriculum that is online or on CD. He usually does this until 4:00 or so.

—Connie Ajay

Ian's Schedule

We use a large dry erase board with a line for every hour of the day. We start the schedule by writing in all the fixed classes that Ian must attend that day. Then I ask him if he has anything that is due that day or the next day. These are the priorities. He does the harder cognitive subjects at his

(Continued)

time of best alertness, which is morning. He does physical things at times when his thinking is more disorganized, which is after 4:00.

Homeschool starts at 8:00 A.M. We do every subject every day and usually in the same order. He is in high school and has seven subjects plus math and chemistry labs on Tuesday and Thursday; piano and speech therapy on Wednesday; and literature on Friday with his grandmother. He spends 30–45 minutes on a subject unless he is making progress and wants to finish. This happens more often than you would think. I want him to take a break, and he begs to keep working.

At lunch time (which is usually one hour) I often have my son make his own lunch, and we count it as Home Economics. Other chores such as setting the table, washing the dishes, and lighting a fire in the fireplace are counted as Home Economics activities also. Lunch can also be a time to talk about his favorite topic or about the history he is studying or just read in a book.

Other activities that fill Ian's day include 40–60 minutes of piano practice. He has taken piano lessons for eight years. Sometimes he jams on the piano as a stress release. P.E. consists of a two-mile walk with our two dogs. If it is raining, he does exercises from a checklist or we go to the YMCA to work out or swim. When we go hiking, biking, or skiing on the weekends, we also count these activities as P.E. hours.

By 5:00 he is really ready to quit. His younger sister comes home from school, and they watch teen sitcoms until dinner. The sitcoms are kind of corny, but he does learn a little about teen interaction. It is something that he and his sister like to do together to defuse after school.

—Ann Coe

16 | How Can Parents Address Behavioral Issues?

Understanding why behavior is happening is the most critical component of positive behavior management. This is often difficult to assess during the heat of the moment. Parents can lose objectivity about their children's behavior, and it is difficult to remove the emotion from the situation. There is a fairly simple process that parents can use to help objectively determine the *why* of challenging behavior. Once this is done, a system can be put in place to help prevent and correct the problematic behavior in a highly supportive and positive way called Positive Behavior Support Plan. A parent can go through this process themselves using the steps described below or can secure the assistance of a behavior specialist or psychologist.

The process of determining why a behavior is occurring is called Functional Behavior Assessment (FBA). Another way to think about the behavior assessment is becoming a *behavior detective.* Like a detective, you are on a quest to solve a mystery, in this case the mystery of the behavior or meltdown. Your job is to find the clues and put the information together until you solve the mystery. Essentially you are looking at what occurs before and after the behavior in order to make your best guess about *why* the behavior is occurring (the function the behavior serves for your child). Looking at the situations that precede the behavior and the outcomes or what follows behavior can give you big clues about the purpose the behavior is serving for your child. Before you become a behavior detective and start the FBA process, it is critical that you examine your own thoughts and beliefs about the behavior. If you enter the process with the wrong frame of mind, you are destined for ongoing frustration. We will take you through *Behavior Detective School* in this next section so you have all the information you need to solve your behavior mystery.

Behavior Detective School: The Five Laws of Behavior

Based on the science of human behavior, we know that certain definitive laws exist that govern human learning and responding. These laws are important to consider when determining why certain patterns of behavior emerge. Here are the five laws of behavior:

Law 1: All behavior happens for a reason.

Law 2: Behavior that is being "reinforced" will continue to occur.

Law 3: If a behavior is responded to inconsistently, it will be harder to change.

Law 4: Punishment does not result in long-term behavior change.

Law 5: Behavior that is learned (even undesired behavior) can be "unlearned."

Now we will explore these laws of behavior in greater detail.

Law 1: All behavior happens for a reason. People engage in behavior either to acquire something that is desired or to escape or avoid something that is disliked or found to be aversive.

Think about your own behavior:

- Why do most adults go to work? Usually it is to earn a paycheck, which then allows us to purchase the things we need and want.

- Why do we tell white lies? Usually we tell white lies to avoid hurting someone else's feelings or to avoid some type of negative consequence.

Your child's behavior is occurring for the same two reasons. It is likely that he is trying to obtain something that he desires, needs, or wants, or perhaps he is attempting to escape or avoid something that is undesired, challenging, or that causes a high level of emotional dysregulation.

There are many common reasons that people with ASD engage in unconventional or problematic behavior. Table 4.2 indicates the functions of behavior that are common for individuals on the Autism Spectrum.

Law 2: Behavior that is being "reinforced" will continue to occur. In other words, if the behavior is working for the child, it will continue to happen. This is a tricky law, because it may not be obvious to the outside observer what the child is getting out of engaging in

Table 4.2. Behavior Functions

Behavior Function: To Get or Obtain	Behavior Function: To Escape or Avoid
Item like a toy, book, or game	A task demand such as getting dressed, cleaning up, or doing an academic task like writing or reading
An activity like the computer, a favorite movie, or time alone	An activity that the child finds frustrating or that he does not understand or see a purpose for
A sensory experience that is exciting or regulating	An activity or setting that may be overstimulating or aversive due to sensory stimulation
An interaction with another person for help, clarification of expectation, or assistance with emotional regulation	An interaction with another person, a social interaction that he may not understand, or an interaction with a person with whom he has a negative history

the behavior. It is only through observing and being a detective that one can figure out the "reinforcer." Keep in mind, too, that a reinforcer is not the same thing as a reward, which we use to increase desirable behaviors and enhance motivation. A reinforcer is anything that follows a behavior that influences that behavior to occur again in the future. Simply put, if the behavior is continuing to happen, something is reinforcing its use.

Law 3: If a behavior is inconsistently responded to, it will be much harder to change. The easiest way to think about this law is to consider a slot machine and how the inconsistent and unpredictable payouts often result in a high level of persistence. The players do not want to stop playing because the machine intermittently reinforces them with a payout. Behaviors such as tantrums respond in the same way to inconsistent consequences. It is much harder to eliminate tantrums and other undesired behaviors when they are being "paid off," sometimes by inconsistent consequences.

Law 4: Punishment does not result in long-term behavior change. Nor does it address the necessary learning of a better, more socially acceptable way to get things we want or avoid things we find uncomfortable. Punishment can only result in the temporary stoppage of an undesired behavior, not a long-term change for the better. Long-term change means teaching better, more prosocial behaviors. This can take a while, but is the answer to behavior problems in the long run. It is also important to consider some of the undesired side effects of punishment. Oftentimes there is a generalized effect; the child learns to avoid engaging in the behavior that was punished but also begins to avoid the punisher or person who administered the punitive consequence. It is awfully difficult to teach a child if he spends his time actively avoiding interactions.

Law 5: Behavior that is learned (even undesired behavior) can be "unlearned." New behaviors can be learned to replace the behavior problems. In other words, *you are not stuck with the current behavior pattern!* The most effective way to change a troublesome behavior is to teach the child a more acceptable alternative behavior that will meet that same need for him or her. Sometimes this means teaching the child to ask for a break or help rather than storming off in order to escape or avoid a difficult task.

Now that you have learned the laws of behavior, you can begin to reflect on your situation and become a behavior detective.

Depersonalize and Put on Your Detective Gear

To be a good behavior detective, you must realize that your child is most likely not engaging in the behavior just to upset you. Most children with ASD lack the sophistication in Theory of Mind (ToM), perspective taking skills, or organizational thinking necessary to develop an elaborate plan of behavior designed specifically to annoy another person. Although many with Asperger Syndrome or high-functioning autism become curious about the effect their behaviors have on others (much like cause and effect), usually the intent of their behavior is not about inflicting a negative emotional reaction on others. They may be protesting a demand or attempting to gain an interaction with someone who can help them regulate their frustration. This is a different motivation from acting out in an attempt to annoy or retaliate against someone else. Keeping in mind the nature of this disability and the differences in what motivates the behavior of people with ASD is critical in solving the mystery of a behavior or meltdown.

Begin the Detective Work with a Functional Behavior Assessment (FBA)

As you begin the assignment to solve a behavior mystery, we encourage you to take a few days to gather some data. Use a journal to keep track of the behaviors and follow the steps described here to gather the clues to solve the behavior mystery.

Step 1: Define the behavior. Start with a very specific definition of the behavior you are concerned about and wish to target for change. Try to define it as descriptively as possible. For example, rather than targeting "meltdowns," try to specifically describe the behavior as you see your child acting through his escalation from the earliest signs of anger or frustration to the highest. For example, turns red, begins to use a loud voice, escalates to yelling and saying profanities, and can continue to a level of hitting the wall or other people. Defining the behaviors as you see them and attempting to define the "escalation pattern" is very helpful in developing your plan of intervention. Typically, the earlier in the escalation pattern you are able to intervene, the better. If you have not defined this pattern, you may miss the golden opportunity to prevent the escalation and teach self-regulation.

Step 2: Describe the precursors to the behavior. Try to identify those times, demands, situations, and conditions that are typically triggers for the behavior. This may take several days of careful observation and recording. When you are able to identify the triggers, you can begin to plan your prevention strategies and will know where to focus your accommodations or change the presentation of a particular demand. In addition, many children can benefit from self-awareness training. This includes teaching them to recognize their triggers and providing them with strategies for coping and self-advocacy. For example, if your child is commonly upset when given lengthy verbal directions, he could learn to recognize this trigger and state to others, "I don't do well with verbal directions, could you please write it down?" or he could say, "Too many words, slow down please."

Step 3: Look at the behavior outcomes. This involves describing and identifying what typically follows the behavior. This should be recorded for a period of a few days to see if there is a consistent pattern. Remember that if the behavior is continuing to occur, the child is getting something from it. The best clues about what your child is getting out of the behavior come from looking at the outcomes of the behavior. For example, if every time a child yells and screams, "I can't do this, it is too hard!" an adult comes to his assistance and helps him break the task down into simple, manageable steps, one can assume that he is yelling in order to access assistance from an adult. This is the "function" the behavior is serving. Once the function is identified, the critical question to answer is what appropriate alternatives can the child use that will access the same outcome. In this case it might be calmly asking an adult for assistance.

Step 4: Solve the behavior mystery. Look at all the clues from Steps 2 and 3 and solve the mystery of the meltdowns. List three possible reasons the behavior may be happening. If you get stuck, refer back to Table 4.2 to see if any of these possible functions fit. Keep in mind that because people with ASD have organizational deficits, they often engage in behavior in order to access help or more specific instructions from others. They also require a higher level of support and mediation from others to regulate their emotions and often engage in problematic behavior when they are frustrated in order to access help with emotional regulation. Parents are very good at becoming the regulators of their children's emotions. This purpose is different from indicating, "He is just doing it for attention." You really must look at what the attention is providing for the child. In the case of ASD, it is not typical that they are engaging in behavior merely for the social interaction it provides. The interaction is likely giving them something that they need and cannot access alone or independently.

After a few days of careful observation and recording of your child's behavior, complete the Behavior Detective forms at the end of this section and solve your behavior mystery. These forms should help you figure out why the behavior is occurring.

Develop Your Positive Behavior Support Plan

The final phase of your detective work is developing a plan for how to change the behavior. This process involves the development of a Positive Behavior Support Plan. It is quite easy to develop a plan to change the behavior once you have gathered all the clues. Now that you have a clearer picture of the behavior and some ideas about *why* it may be occurring, you are ready to develop a plan.

The Positive Behavior Support Plan should include the following elements in order to be most effective:

1. Prevention strategies and accommodations.

2. Teaching plan for the alternative and compensatory skills, including how they will be taught and rewarded.

3. A plan for how to respond to the behavior at low levels or when escalation has just begun and a reactive strategy or plan for responding once the behavior has escalated. Hopefully the behavior won't escalate if Steps 1 and 2 are implemented.

4. Strategies for behavioral reflection and problem solving that will teach your child to evaluate his own behavior. This type of self-reflection may not be appropriate for younger children or those with significant cognitive delays.

Start with a prevention plan. This involves looking at and evaluating the triggers for the behavior. We have found that there are some common things that tend to trigger problematic behaviors in individuals with ASD. These are fairly predictable antecedents that, due to the inherent sensory, social, and communication differences of individuals with ASD, are relatively sure to result in trouble.

- *Unexpected or too much sensory input.* Often our children are startled or taken off guard when they encounter unexpected sensory input like a loud noise, a highly visually stimulating or active environment, or a very strong smell or odor. Because of the differences in the sensory system and the inability to cope with a high level of sensory input, children with ASD may react by engaging in a maladaptive behavior. This behavior is often an attempt to escape or avoid this unpleasant experience, or it is an attempt to secure some support in coping with or handling the experience.

- *Expectations are unclear or different from what the child expected.* Because children with ASD prefer to follow learned routines and rules and lack the cognitive flexibility to adjust quickly to changes, they often react when the expectations change. The adult may think they have made the schedule or expectations clear, but the child may have had a different plan in mind. The unexpected change may result in a behavioral reaction from the child, or he may engage in behaviors in an attempt to change the routine back to what he knows or is comfortable with.

- *Tasks are not functional or interesting to the child.* If the child is not interested in the topic or learning about a particular thing, he may protest or engage in unconventional behaviors to avoid the task demand.

- *Expectations are above the child's ability level.* They can be too difficult either academically or organizationally (the task has too many steps and has not been broken down enough). Sometimes the way the information or task is presented can trigger a behavior if the task seems too big or if the child does not believe that he knows how to do it. We all like to do things that we are good at, and new challenges often elicit fear or anxiety. These feelings can be compounded in children with ASD, resulting in overreactions to seemingly simple task demands.

- *Attempts at communication have gone unnoticed.* Perhaps the child has attempted to ask for help or clarification, but these lower-level behaviors or requests have not been responded to. The child may escalate his behaviors as his frustration or anxiety increases. This escalation can occur very rapidly in many children with ASD, as they lack the ability to wait for support.

- *Too much information has been given at one time.* Often when the information has been provided orally rather than in a more visual or written format, it causes problems. Because of the deficits many children with ASD have in their auditory working memory, they are not able to keep track of or hold onto information that is presented orally. This can lead to frustration or behaviors that then ultimately give them access to more support or information to clarify the task demands.

- *Instructions are above the child's language level.* This can be a problem even if the child has a great vocabulary. Many children with ASD interpret language literally and do not understand things like idioms, figures of speech, or sarcasm.

This can often result in frustration or confusion. They may act out in frustration or may misinterpret the communication and simply make a mistake.

- *The child is distracted by other sensory issues.* He may miss the instructions or only hear part of them. Because it is very challenging for children with ASD to filter out incoming sensory information and they can often only pay attention to one thing at a time, they miss important information. This, at times, looks like "noncompliance" or willful disobedience to adult directions.

There are many things that you can do to prevent the occurrence of problematic behavior. Now that you have some ideas about what the triggers are, here are some ideas to consider for preventing the problems:

- *Structure and prepare the environment ahead of time.* It is also helpful to provide a higher level of visual information. Highly organized and structured learning and working environments are very regulating to individuals who lack the innate ability to organize themselves. Visual organization provides additional clarity about expectations and helps visual learners like those with ASD know what to do.

- *Reward good behavior and functional communication.* It is important that we focus on the positive when it does occur and provide very specific verbal praise such as, "I really like the way you asked me for help with a calm, quiet voice." This points out to the child what the expected behavior is and helps to establish this as the appropriate behavior that will get consistent rewards.

- *Use clear, simple directions and provide visual support whenever possible.* This will help eliminate miscommunications and will provide the child with the concrete reference of a visual instruction to compensate for the auditory working memory deficits common to those with ASD.

- *Create a predictable schedule and routine.* This is important to establish so that the child knows and understands the expectations. Consistency often provides a level of comfort and contributes to emotional regulation. However, you want to take advantage of the fact that you can have a higher level of flexibility when homeschooling, as compared to traditional school. Acknowledging that children with ASD must be taught how to accept and cope with changes should intentionally build flexibility lessons into the daily routine. This is a very important skill that can be taught in a systematic and carefully planned way. As a general rule, schedules and routines should be fairly consistent. Changes should be made in advance using visual information that is appropriate for the child. This gives the child with ASD concrete visual information, time to adjust to the change, and an opportunity to prepare for the upcoming event.

- *Incorporate appropriate sensory activities throughout the day.* Opportunities to access movement and exercise or other sensory regulating activities are a critical part of a program for most individuals with ASD. These activities should be individualized to meet the needs of the child. They can include things like swinging, walking, swimming, or doing stretches or yoga. If your child is younger or has fewer self-management skills, you can facilitate sensory activities such as massage, applying form pressure touch, or other regulating activities. There are many resources available to assist a parent in developing a sensory motor program, including *The Out of Sync Child Has Fun: Activities for Kids with Sensory Integration Dysfunction, Asperger's Syndrome and Sensory Issues: Practical*

Solutions for Making Sense of the World, and *Answers to Questions Teachers Ask About Sensory Integration: Forms, Checklists, and Practical Tools for Teachers and Parents*.[19] You can also access support and consultation from an occupational therapist who is trained in Sensory Integration Therapy.

- *Teach the child acceptable ways to communicate likes, dislikes, and needs.* Many children with ASD lack the verbal communication skills to access the things that they need or want. This in and of itself results in the use of unconventional behaviors. For nonverbal or preverbal children, implementing a functional communication system such as the Picture Exchange Communication System (PECS) can have dramatic results.[20] Even more highly verbal children and those with Asperger's Syndrome may require explicit instruction in some functional communication skills such as asking for help, a break from work or demands, or support with self-regulation. Two Web sites that offer information, activities, and products to address sensory processing needs in children that may be helpful to parents and teachers are the following:

S'cool Moves: www.schoolmoves.com/index.html

Brain Gym: www.braingym.com

- *Make sure you use appropriate accommodations for your child's sensory needs.* If you know that your child has a difficult time coping with loud or unexpected noises, perhaps using noise-blocking headphones could help when out in the community or in environments where this is likely to occur. If fluorescent lighting is troublesome, wearing sunglasses or a brimmed hat could provide just enough of a filter to prevent problems. If unexpected touch causes discomfort, wearing thicker layers of clothing can provide a needed barrier. These extra layers of clothing could be called "under-armor" protection from unexpected touch. Again, you can consult with an occupational therapist to determine other "blocking" techniques that might help with these sensory issues.

• *Provide opportunities for choice whenever possible.* This is a relatively easy technique to incorporate into daily life. Choice can be between activities, such as, "Do you want to do math first or spelling?", between locations, for instance, "Do you want to work at the table or the desk?", or between starting and ending points, for example, "Do you want to do questions 1–5 or 6–10?" Choice provides an opportunity to create shared control and often build both buy-in to the task and trust in the educational relationship.

• *Make learning meaningful to your child.* Obviously, if the child sees the importance and buys into the learning experience you are likely to encounter fewer behaviors. This is a huge benefit in homeschooling. It affords you the opportunity for greater creativity in the design of your lessons and allows you to teach within a natural and functional context with frequent opportunities for generalization of skills. If you find that you are continually encountering problems around a specific type of learning activity or subject, brainstorm alternative ways of teaching or addressing this skill. Talk to other families about how they have taught the skill or simply give it a rest and come back to it at a later date. Often a break is all that is necessary in order to alleviate frustration.

Look at the triggers for your behavior and the ideas we have provided and develop your own prevention plan. Use the Focus on Prevention forms provided for you at the end of this section to guide you through this process.

Parent Perspective

Sometimes, behaviors appear more with the parent than a more neutral party, and certain "trigger" subjects or activities may be best taught through an online class, DVD "teacher," paid tutor, friend, homeschool co-op, or classroom setting, if possible.

—Karen Crum

The replacement behavior. This is the most challenging yet most critical part of your plan. You now have to identify a behavior or set of behaviors that your child can do to replace the problematic ones, but these behaviors have to get your child the same results! So if you hypothesize that your child is using the behavior to escape math, he or she has to learn a better behavior that will allow them to escape math. Additionally, you need to be asking how to approach math in a different way, so that it does not elicit the strong desire to escape it. This relates back to the prevention strategies discussed above.

The replacement behavior:

- Must serve the same function or purpose for the child as the problematic behavior does
- Must be as efficient as the behavior it is replacing
- Can be a known behavior or one that the child is already using under different circumstances
- Must be taught, practiced, and rewarded heavily

There are many skill deficits that are common among people with ASD that we have seen contribute to the occurrence of problematic behavior. As you are thinking about your child's behavior, determine if one or more of these skills need to be taught in order to replace the problematic behavior you are targeting for change.

- *Identifying and requesting desired items and activities.* Because language and expressive communication are often impaired in ASD, many children do not have an effective way of being able to communicate even the basic needs for food, something to drink, or access to activities or items they need or want. These children (and adults) must resort to getting the needed items for themselves or using unconventional behavior to get them. When functional communication is taught either through pictures, sign language, or other augmentative systems, behavior problems are sure to subside. Asking for a *break* from a highly stressful activity and asking for *assistance or help* are the two most common skill deficits observed in students with high-functioning autism. The child may possess the language skills to make these requests, but is not using them at the appropriate times or before he reaches the point of no return—when the frustration overrides the ability to use words to get the needs met. Visual strategies can assist even highly verbal children in learning how to request help and break appropriately (see Figure 4.16 a and b).

- *Communicating sensory needs or the need for regulatory input.* The child may recognize that something is bothering him, but is not able to put it into words. He uses escape or avoidance behaviors to eliminate the aversive input, but may not be able to describe the need to others in a way that makes sense. Additionally, the child may be using unconventional means to

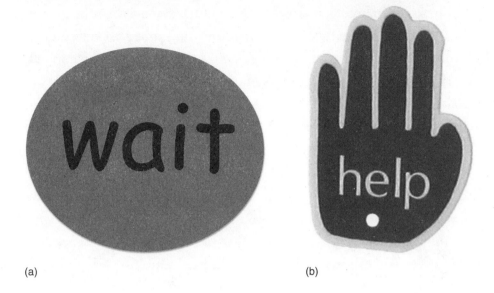

(a)   (b)

Figure 4.16.   (a) Break and (b) Help Cards

provide self-regulation whenever he is upset or uncomfortable. For example, the child may be chewing his pencil when nervous or anxious. This type of oral stimulation can be quite calming, but when he is prompted to stop (perhaps because he has made a mess or there is a danger of splinters), he escalates to having tantrums. The child needs to learn to identify his sensory triggers and must be taught more appropriate strategies for self-calming, coping, and self-regulation. As mentioned above, the child may be using unconventional behaviors to help with regulation. Often our kids must be taught strategies for self-calming that can be used in public settings, and that are socially appropriate. These can include counting, deep breathing, and positive self-talk. In the case of chewing on a pencil, the student may have permission to chew gum or have open access to crunchy foods such as carrots. Other appropriate chew objects may be recommended by an occupational therapist.

There are many strategies for teaching the replacement behaviors that your child needs to learn. You will now need to develop an individualized plan for teaching the replacement skills that will work for your child given his cognitive ability and learning style. Make sure to include in your teaching plan a highly motivating reward for using the replacement behavior. Think of the replacement skill as a *high-priority* skill, because without learning it your child will continue to use the problematic behavior. Recognize that it will take time for your child to learn and use this new skill, and there may be some "unlearning" or habit breaking that must occur along with learning the new skill. Most important, trust that you can teach this skill just as you can teach other more academic and functional skills.

Commonsense reactive strategies. The best way to handle any behavior problem is to prevent it from occurring in the first place; however, there will certainly be times where this is just not possible. Catching your child at the lowest levels of escalation is desired because this is a time where he can easily be redirected to engage in the replacement behavior. Looking for those telltale signs that there is a problem and simply redirecting your child to ask for help, a break, or to communicate what he needs or wants can be highly effective if you are a good observer. If you miss the signs, which are likely to happen on occasion, the following are some commonsense ways of responding to the behavior. Please notice that these are not "punishments"; they are ways of minimizing possible reinforcement while keeping the child and your self safe and sound.

- *Responding to aggression.* Calmly give corrective feedback to your child such as "Stop, hands down." Make sure others are safe in the area, or remove others from the area when necessary. When appropriate, reinforce others who are acting appropriately. Use an appropriate "hands-on" strategy only when necessary to keep the child safe. For example, carry the child to his room, redirect him to another area, or remove yourself from the situation if necessary. If aggression increases abruptly and for no apparent reason, we advise consulting with a physician to rule out any medical issues that could be underlying.

- *Responding to self-injurious behaviors.* First, don't overreact. If it really hurts, most likely your child will stop. If you overreact, you might accidentally reinforce that behavior. You can provide your child with calm, but firm, corrective feedback, such as "Hands down, you are okay." Make sure your child is safe, which may include using an appropriate "hands on" strategy such as moving him to a quiet area or a soft surface. If you have to do this, try not to overindulge your child with attention. If the child is really seriously injuring himself or has the potential to do so, you must stop the behavior. We would also advise you to consult immediately with your child's physician, as this kind of self-injury or severe aggression could be indicating some other kind of health issue.

- *Responding to noncompliance.* First, remind your child of the reward he is working for or the next activity that you will be doing. Sometimes it helps to provide a visual or something in writing to maintain the motivation. For example, "first math, then swimming" could be written on a whiteboard and placed next to the child. Ignore noncompliant verbalization and keep a calm physical demeanor. Allow time for your child to regroup and regain control, and do not provide a great deal of attention when this is occurring. Prompt your child through the task or at least a final step, so that you end on your terms and hopefully on a successful note. Do not allow your child access to the next activity or reward until he follows through with your request or part of it. Don't forget to reinforce any and all compliance, even if it is with a bit of attitude.

- *Responding to tantrums.* Even though it may be difficult, try to ignore all of the child's self-indulgent behavior. Allow your child time to regroup and clam down. Reinforce immediately as soon as the tantrums are discontinued or appropriate behavior is displayed.

- *Responding to self-stimulation.* Ignore or interrupt a child's behavior by either verbally or physically prompting him. Redirect the child to a meaningful or engaging activity. Recognize that your child may be overstimulated by the current activity and events and offer to change the activity if possible

Behavioral reflection. Many children can benefit from an opportunity to reflect on their behavior after the fact in order to learn from it and problem solve different ways of handling the situation in the future. Behavioral reflection can provide your child with a way of learning in context about his triggers, his emotions, and the impact his behavior has on others. Some children can be taken through behavioral reflection with verbal counseling; however, most children with ASD need to have some visual support added to this process. We have found it very effective to use a graphic organizer or thinking tool to systematically walk a child with ASD through behavioral reflection. Refer back to Question 13 and Figures 4.6 through 4.9 for more on thinking tools.

Parent Perspective

Most of his tantrums are due to feeling overwhelmed. I have learned to avoid "throwing fuel on the fire" and to just wait out the tantrums, and then when he is calm, discuss them with him.

—Ann Coe

Essentially, you are teaching the child to be his own behavior detective and to solve his own mystery of the meltdown. A word of advice: it is equally important to have your child reflect on behaviors that are positive or that had a good outcome for him. If you only reflect when things go wrong, you are missing valuable opportunities to help your child learn about his talents, strengths, gifts, and accomplishments.

When Can You Expect to See the Behavior Change?

By conducting the functional behavior assessment and developing a strategic Positive Behavior Support Plan, you should begin to see changes within a couple of weeks. The changes may start out slowly, and you may have trouble recognizing that things are moving in a positive direction. Don't give up; change takes time, and it is important that you are being very consistent—remember the example of the slot machine. You may even experience what a behavior specialist might call an extinction burst. That is when things get a little bit worse before they improve, as your child gives a last-ditch effort to make the old behavior pattern work. Stay with your plan and ride out this extinction burst. It can help to continue keeping your behavior log, as this will provide you with a more objective way of looking at the behavior. You can add up the number of times the behavior occurred prior to your Positive Behavior Support Plan and then the number of times it occurred three weeks after you begin implementing the plan.

If you are not seeing results after a month, you may need to adjust the plan or do more detective work. You may also want to talk with someone from your personal support network. Sometimes it just takes a "new set of eyes" to see a change that has not been obvious to you. If all else fails, call in the professionals to give you some ideas, strategies, or tips. It might be a simple little adjustment to your plan that will make all the difference in the world.

Behavior Detective Form 1

Solve the Mystery of the Meltdown

Antecedents: What are the situations, times, activities, demands, instructions, people, or events that appear to precede the behavior?

Behavior: What is your child doing that is not appropriate for that situation?

Consequences: What happens following the behavior or as a result of the behavior?

Behavior Detective Form 1

Solve the Mystery of the Meltdown

(Sample)

Antecedents: What are the situations, times, activities, demands, instructions, people, or events that appear to precede the behavior?

Refusal and protesting often occur when Ollie is asked to read science, history, or literature books by himself (independent reading). This can occur at any time in the day, but is worse in the afternoons. Ollie will not refuse to read his comic books or gaming magazines.

Behavior: What is your child doing that is not appropriate for that situation?

Instead of completing the reading assigned to him, Ollie fidgets with his pencil and refuses to read the chapter. He often protests loudly, saying things like "I hate this book, I hate my life!" "Why do I have to learn about this, it is dumb!"

Consequences: What happens following the behavior or as a result of the behavior?

When Ollie refuses to read, I will typically encourage him, offer him a desired activity if he finishes his reading, or I will sit and read with him.

Behavior Detective Form 2

Mind Reading

Possible Functions the Behavior Serves:

Identify the top 3 reasons your child might be engaging in this behavior:

Reason 1:

Reason 2:

Reason 3:

Skill(s) Needing to Be Learned:

Strategies You Might Use to Teach and Reinforce These Skills:

Behavior Detective Form 2

Mind Reading

(SAMPLE)

Possible Functions the Behavior Serves:

Identify the top 3 reasons your child might be engaging in this behavior:

Reason 1: *To escape or avoid reading things he does not find interesting or appealing.*
Reason 2: *To get an interaction with me that helps him to regulate his emotional displeasure about the assignment and maintain his attention to the task at hand.*
Reason 3: *To get 1:1 attention from me.*

Skill(s) Needing to Be Learned:

Skill 1: *Ollie needs to ask for a break or a new assignment.*
Skill 2: *Ollie needs to ask for help or to self-regulate his attention and emotional arousal states using self-regulation strategies.*
Skill 3: *Ollie needs to ask for attention and interactions with me in a socially acceptable and appropriate manner, such as, "Mom, can you read this with me?"*

Strategies You Might Use to Teach and Reinforce These Skills:

Skill 1: *Ollie could learn to use a break card or break-ticket system. I could give him a certain number to use at his discretion throughout the day.*
Skill 2: *Ollie could learn to use a help card or a help-ticket system to get interactions with me for support.*
Skills 3: *Ollie could learn to do deep breathing or stretching to help with self-regulation. He could use a 5-point scale to indicate his level of frustration and things that can help him to calm and regulate himself.*

Behavior Detective Form 3

Focus on Prevention

Determine the Likely Triggers for Your Child's Behavior:

Determine Some Preventative Strategies to Try:

How Can You Accommodate Sensory Differences?

How Can You Provide More Visual Support and Structure?

Behavior Detective Form 3

Focus on Prevention

(SAMPLE)

Determine the Likely Triggers for Your Child's Behavior:

The likely triggers for Ollie's protesting and refusal are the subject area that he is being assigned to read about, a low-interest subject area.

Determine Some Preventative Strategies To Try:

Allow Ollie to participate in designing the lessons in science, history, and literature so they incorporate his interests.

 Allow Ollie to watch films, movies, or multimedia presentations about the topics we are covering

 Break the reading up into small chunks using a visual indicator such as an arrow sticker, and allow Ollie a few minutes of break time after a small interval of reading

 Allow Ollie to preselect a reward he wants to earn for completing his reading assignments each day.

How Can You Accommodate Sensory Differences?

Prepare Ollie for these sedentary activities by doing something highly physical before and after.

How Can You Provide More Visual Support and Structure?

Use a visual reinforcement system that states, "First read 10 pages, then earn some Nintendo time." Use visual indicators of quantity to show Ollie when he earns a break.

17 | How Can Parents Determine the Appropriate Accommodations and Modifications That Are Necessary for Curricular Success?

The answer to this question begins with a question: what exactly are accommodations and modifications? Some students with disabilities need accommodations or modifications to their educational program in order to participate in the general curriculum and to be successful in school. While the Individuals with Disabilities Education Act (IDEA) and its regulations do not define accommodations or modifications, there is some agreement as to what they mean.

It is generally accepted that an *accommodation* allows a student to complete the same assignment or test as other students, but with a change in the timing, formatting, setting, scheduling, response, and/or presentation. An accommodation does not alter in any significant way what the test or assignment measures. An accommodation often means adding additional conditions or favorable circumstances or removing barriers to success that will allow the student to demonstrate a skill which is measured in the same way as it is for the same-aged peer.

A *modification* typically means an adjustment to an assignment or a test that changes the standard or what the test or assignment is supposed to measure. It does lower the difficulty or instructional level of the skill, and can often be a completely alternative assignment or curriculum from that of the same-aged peers.

Although these two terms are often used interchangeably, they do not mean the same thing. In a traditional school setting where a student has an Individual Educational Program (IEP), it is the responsibility of the IEP team (including parents) to determine the necessary accommodations, modifications, or both. Many parents we have interviewed express frustration in the lack of willingness of some educators to implement the stated accommodations or modifications in traditional school settings. Often, the lack of implementation stems from a lack of understanding of these terms, how to implement them, and how to measure the student's progress. Some parents have stated that educating their child at home has provided them with the freedom to naturally accommodate the child's needs, pace, and learning style. This freedom has minimized the need for specifically stated accommodations or modifications.

Parents who have chosen public or public charter homeschool programs typically have regular meetings with a homeschool teacher who will assist them in either accommodating or modifying assignments as appropriate to their child's needs. The parent, teacher, and student, as appropriate, will determine what accommodations

Parent Perspective

In homeschool your child can have all the accommodations that you can squeeze into the day. He can have one-on-one learning, downtime when needed, a quiet environment, more time on tests, oral testing, a flexible schedule, the option of taking fewer classes, more years of school while still getting good grades, the use of special interest for motivation, and the opportunity to use specialized curriculum such as *Learning the R.O.P.E.S. for Improved Executive Functioning* (Schetter, 2004) consistently throughout his day.

—Ann Coe

> ## Parent Perspective
>
> I really needed help from my son's charter homeschool facilitator and the special education teacher to establish this. I didn't want to accommodate him more than was necessary, thinking that he might not be able to fit back into a classroom for college. I think you need to look at the places where the student is not successful; then try to figure out why, and then think of things that would help bring about success.
>
> —Ann Coe

and modifications to use. It is very important to include the child in this process as it establishes the foundation for understanding personal learning needs and how to advocate for himself as he transitions to college or the workforce.

The following list of ideas for accommodations and modifications may be helpful in supporting a student's learning style and needs. Accommodations that may be helpful in the home include the following:

Quantity
- Shorten task or assignments by giving fewer items.
- Chunk the assignment into manageable parts.
- Ask the student how much he thinks he can finish in the designated time; negotiate as needed to get a reasonable amount completed.

Parent Perspective

In Algebra my son works very slowly. He is not interested in math, and he is not very intuitive. The first problem was simply to get him to do the work with a positive attitude. We did this by setting obtainable goals such as to do five problems. They were corrected right away, so there was immediate feedback. We used lots of praise and went over any that were incorrect.

—Ann Coe

Parent Perspective

We spend more time on the parts that are difficult for him and breeze through anything that he understands quickly. He spends about two hours on weekends doing math and an hour a day during vacations. He is used to this now and would rather do a little a day instead of being totally overwhelmed by a whole problem set.

—Ann Coe

Time

- Give additional time to complete a task.
- Require less time to work on frustrating or difficult tasks.
- Schedule frequent breaks.
- Make time visual by using any of the following: Time Timer, a digital timer, or a sand hourglass.

Parent Perspective

The Internet provides plenty of Web sites that can provide types of accommodations and modifications in order for the student to understand the instruction. Additionally, there are plenty of curriculums or modules that are available to be used.

—Connie Ajay

Input

- Provide visual supports, such as graphic organizers, highlighters, and so on.
- Provide written directions, to-do lists, or task lists.
- Provide books on tape.
- Use manipulatives and hands-on activities.
- Provide concrete samples.
- Expand topic with input from experts in the community, online, or other media.

Output

- Allow verbal rather than written responses.
- Allow the student to demonstrate knowledge via hands-on projects.
- Allow tape-recorded responses for assignments.
- Use the computer and keyboard for assignments.
- Evaluate or grade the student on the process instead of the product.

Parent Perspective

I break the tests up into four to five parts and have him study for each part just before taking the test. He doesn't take the test until he is ready. He passed the California High School Exit Examination the first time he took it as a tenth grader.

—Ann Coe

Level of Support

- Provide instructional support as required, ranging from direct instruction to independent exploration as appropriate to the child.

- Use visual timers to support time management.

- Provide a graphic organizer to assist in prioritizing the importance of tasks.

- Create a self-management chart to train for self-regulation and independence.

- Facilitate group learning with peers.

Other Possible Accommodations

- Develop a menu of positive *reinforcers* (rewards) with the child and determine a plan for systematic use. *Important reminder:* a reinforcer (reward) is not a bribe. A reward is determined before work begins by asking, "What are you working for when you finish your assignment?" If a student's motivation lags, a simple reminder of what he is working for may remotivate him. It is a bribe if the student is not working and a reward is offered to get him motivated to finish the work. One must also remember that reinforcers do not always maintain the same value to any individual, and this is especially true of a child with ASD. To ensure that reinforcers continue to hold their value, one should check in regularly with the child either by asking them or offering choices prior to an assigner task. The systematic use of reinforcement is a vital component to any program either at home or in the traditional school setting. A very simple explanation of schedules of reinforcement can be found on the Wikipedia Web site at http://en.wikip edia.org/wiki/Reinforcement.

- Set up a specific study office or school area that sets the environmental mood for learning when there is a need for quiet sustained attention with limited distracters.

- Develop personalized homeschool rules or guidelines. The shift from parent to teacher can be challenging, but if there are guidelines this may be more easily understood.

When a family is homeschooling a child who has cognitive delays and autism, program and instructional modifications are

Parent Perspective

Parents need to educate themselves about autism so they can implement the most "tried-and-true" accommodations for children with autism first. Parents *must* have these resources to consult if they get into a bind in order for homeschooling to continue to be a positive experience.

—Karen Crum

typically used. For these children, meeting the typical academic standard is not the expected outcome. Modifications that may be helpful at home include

Difficulty Reduction

- Use a calculator for math. This would not be a reduction in difficulty if a specific calculator is required for higher-level math.

- Use materials that are below the child's grade level, such as a high-interest, low-vocabulary book on electricity for science.

- If testing is part of the curriculum, allow the child to use notes or an open book to complete the test.

- Allow the child to use a graphic organizer to complete an assignment that requires an essay rather than write it in standard format.

- Determine an alternate method to demonstrate growth and progress.

Alternate Goals

- A child may have a reading goal; however, the content is life-skills-based with the child learning to read words that are relevant in his world, as opposed to a literature-based reading program.

- Partial participation in an activity may be the goal, as opposed to full participation. For example, a child may just stir a cake mix while the parent, sibling, or peer read the recipe, measure, and complete the other steps when making a cake.

Substitute Curriculum

- The curriculum is based on the life skills that the child needs to function as independently as possible now and as an adult. The basic language, academic, motor, and social skills are imbedded in relevant meaningful daily activities. An example (see Table 4.3) demonstrates how a visit to a fast food restaurant can be an excellent teaching environment to work on every basic skill with a highly motivating reward, lunch, after instruction.

Many of the accommodations and modifications listed are implemented very naturally by parents, whether they are in the role of teacher or parent. However, it is helpful to define what is actually being done to assist the child in learning the skills to become the best adult possible. Support is very important, but teaching for independence is the ultimate goal; thus, attention must be given to the type of support being provided.

Table 4.3. Substitute Curriculum

Task	Skill	Goal
Stands in line to place order	Social	Maintain appropriate personal space
Place order	Social	Establish eye contact with the cashier
	Language	Place order either verbally or with a picture
Pay for order	Academics	Count number of dollar bills, plus an extra dollar for the change
	Motor	Take money out of wallet
	Social	Establish eye contact with the cashier
		Put out hand for change
Picks up order	Language	Listen for order number
	Academic	Recognize (match) order number
	Motor	Carry tray to the table

Parents (like educators) need to become "a student of the child" to figure out if the child is confused about instructions, overwhelmed about the amount of work in front of them, unsure how to start, afraid of failure, uncomfortable (or too comfortable) in their environment, and so on. Parents also can get a list of possible modifications to try from books, conferences, consulting with local school special educators, other home-schooling parents, and online resources.

—Karen Crum

5

Questions About Transition

18 When Should Parents Consider a Transition Back to Traditional Educational Settings or Programs and How Is This Done?

Just as choosing to homeschool is a parental decision, so is returning to traditional school. The reasons for making the return to traditional school and how this should be accomplished are also varied. Some of the common reasons from the child's point of view include boredom or missing friends. From a parental perspective, the reasons may include that they have taken their child as far as they can, outside opinions have swayed them, or the safety or dissatisfaction that prompted a change to homeschooling has been remediated. For some families, thoughts of transition do not occur until the child is ready to enter college or enter full-time employment. Steps to prepare for these specific transitions will be discussed in Question 20.

Parent Perspective

A transition back to public education part- or full-time may be warranted if the parent and child want the child to attend college in the near future. It may be argued that it is wise to expose the child to the pressures and irritations of traditional school in order to prepare him or her for the real world of postsecondary education.

—Karen Crum

Child Perspectives Regarding Transition

Some children may become bored or tired of the routine of home-school. This situation in and of itself is not necessarily a reason to return to traditional school. It may require parents to look at the underlying motivation issues. In addressing this situation, a parent may want to revisit the child's interest and try to spark life back into the program. Reviewing the suggestions offered in Question 14 may be helpful.

Some students with ASD enjoy the socialization that can take place on the traditional school campus, but cannot tolerate the large class size or pressure of the pace. Partial participation may be a good option in this case. Parents and school personal should identify activities or periods of the day that allow for social contact. Some examples include weekly lunch bunch, elective classes, participating in clubs or sports teams, or attending field trips. The plans for partial participation on a traditional school campus will need to be negotiated with the school on an individual basis.

Parent Perspective

In my experience, very few kids or parents see value in returning to the traditional education setting full-time. However, transitioning back to traditional school might be needed if the child or parent is very unhappy, the child is not making progress, or if a parent becomes ill or needs to return to work. This problem can sometimes be rectified if a homeschool teacher or tutor is hired.

—Karen Crum

Parent Perspectives Regarding Transition

After a period of time, some parents may begin to feel that they have taken their child as far as they can. The child may need additional supports that the parent feels can best be provided by someone else. The school system may not have had appropriate programs when the parents started homeschooling, which are in place now and would benefit the child.

If parents removed their child due to safety issues on campus such as bullying and teasing, they may find that after a period of homeschooling the student has learned better coping skills and is more prepared to handle the social dynamics on a traditional school campus. They may also find that there are other schools where safety and bullying issues are not as prevalent, thus making a return to a traditional campus a positive move.

Some parents may be influenced by the opinions of educators who say they should return their child to public school for the social options that are available there. As discussed in Questions 11 and 12, socialization can be appropriately addressed through a homeschool program. Advice from the educational experts can cause a conflict for families who have experienced the positive features of homeschooling, yet continue to have concerns that their child might not be getting the level of social interactions necessary to grow and develop relationships. It is possible, when provided with appropriate supports and peer training, for social experiences on a traditional campus to be very positive. Parents must work closely with the school personnel to ensure that the necessary structure, training, and support are available.

Once again, ending homeschooling is a family decision that requires the same effort and research that entering homeschooling required. Talk with other families, visit the school sites and programs that might support the child's unique needs, and seek input from the child. The family and child should be informed consumers

Parent Perspective

Some families find that homeschooling is very successful, but the goal is not to embrace homeschooling for the long haul, rather to learn at home as a means to work on the skills necessary to be successful in the traditional classroom and then to transition back there as the child is ready. The child's unique needs should be considered before any transition takes place. Children with ASD do not have an easy time with transitions in general, so there should be much preparedness and understanding of what is happening and why.

—Janelle Lewis

and make a decision that will address everything that is important to nurture the child to become the best that he or she can be.

Steps Parents and Educators Can Take to Facilitate a Smooth Transition

1. *Parents should make an appointment with the principal of their neighborhood school to discuss the possible transition from homeschool to a traditional classroom.* The neighborhood school is recommended as a starting point. The Individuals with Disabilities in Education Act (IDEA) clearly indicates that children with disabilities should be educated with their nondisabled peers to the greatest extent possible based on assessed needs. If the local neighborhood school does not appear to have the necessary supports and services to meet the student's individual assessed needs, the IEP team will make that determination following additional assessment. If the parent is unsure about the policy in their community, a call to the district office may clear up any questions about school options that are available.

2. *Parents should observe the classrooms that are recommended by the principal or school administrator.* Typically, the initial observations are made by the parent alone. If appropriate, the student should also visit and have input. During the observations, the parent should be looking for environmental and social matches that meet the unique needs of their child. The book *R.E.A.D.Y. for Inclusion* by Kandis Lighthall may be a helpful reference to both parents and educators.[1]

3. *After the assessments and observations are complete, an IEP meeting should be held to address all aspects of the student's needs and develop the steps to transition into the student's new class.*

4. *Consider introducing the student to the campus when other students are not on campus, especially if the student has not been on the campus before.* Ensure that the student can find his class, the restrooms, the cafeteria, the office, and other locations that he will need to use. It is also important for the student to meet his new teacher or teachers. The student should see where his desk will be, where to put his backpack and other items, and where important information is displayed. Basic information that will reduce anxiety regarding the unknown should be covered. Of course, everything cannot be covered, but enough must be previewed to promote a feeling of calm for the student and the staff.

5. *Consider doing Ability Awareness activities in the student's new classroom with his classmates prior to the start of school.* These activities may be structured just to introduce the new student or to disclose information about his needs. This can be accomplished without labeling the disability. A procedural reference book for parents and educators on awareness activities is *What Makes School Great? Friends! Activities to Build Autism Awareness and Develop Friendship* by Kandis Lighthall.[2]

6. *General training for the school staff on Autism Spectrum Disorders, as well as the student's specific needs is strongly encouraged.* It is important to train the entire staff because each staff member will become part of the student's support network. If a paraprofessional will be assisting in the classroom, then it is imperative that they receive additional training along with the general education teacher. Understanding ASD is one of the keys to successful inclusion.

7. *Regular team meetings should be scheduled.* When the student first transitions to the school these meetings may be held on a

weekly basis. They are not IEP meetings and only require participation by key individuals. A typical team meeting includes the general education teacher, parents, and administrator. Other members as appropriate might be the paraprofessional, special educator, speech therapist, school psychologist, behavior specialist, school counselor, occupational therapist, program specialist, the student, or any other staff member who plays a role in the student's school program. Team meetings are not meant to involve a cast of thousands, but should include the key people. The team meetings should be kept to thirty minutes with an agenda that discusses what is working, where the concerns are, how to address the concerns, and who will be responsible for implementing the plan to address the concerns. After the first few weekly meetings, if transition is going well, team meetings can be held monthly and eventually quarterly or as needed. Having meetings regularly scheduled and then canceled if not needed is typically more practical than trying to coordinate several people's schedules.

19 How Should a Family Plan for Transition to College?

Some parents reading this, especially parents of the younger child, may simply be planning for the next day or the next week. They may not be thinking or planning for many years ahead. However, parents of students with ASD should consider that college is a possibility. Parents have reported dynamic growth in their children with ASD as a result of homeschooling. No parent or educator would ever want to impose limits on the possibilities for the future.

Recent reports indicate that more and more universities are welcoming students who have been homeschooled. Jon Reider, a

Parent Perspective

My son is in the sixth grade, and right now I don't have a plan. I don't know how Justin is going to do next week. I take things with Justin one day at a time.

—Michelle King

Stanford University admissions officer, stated: "Homeschoolers bring certain skills, motivation, curiosity, and the capacity to be responsible for their education that high schools don't induce very well".[3] Students with ASD who have been homeschooled will bring many of the same talents, as well as some unique gifts and challenges.

If attending college is a goal for the homeschooled student with or without ASD, plans must begin early. The early plans should include determining the type of college that is right for the student. There are vocational or technical colleges, community colleges, and university or four-year college options to choose from. Making a decision on the type of college will assist the student and parents in planning the courses to be taken in high school. Students who are choosing a four-year college or university should consider a comprehensive program that includes the following:

- Four years of English, including grammar, composition, and literature

- Three years of math, including algebra and geometry

- Three years of science, including biology, physical science, and lab experiences

- Three years of social studies, including U.S. history, government, and economics
- Two years of a foreign language
- Two years (minimum) of elective courses
- One technology course

For some older students attending college is a natural progression, as they already may have been taking a few classes at a community college as a high-school-aged student either through an "open-enrollment program" or with permission granted from the school district or homeschool program.

Typically, students who want to attend college need to have a high school diploma, which includes completing the course work listed above and a certain number of credits. When a homeschool program is connected to a public school or charter school, students are acquiring high school credits toward a diploma. As discussed in Question 4, other types of homeschool programs are accredited and can confer a diploma, or at least maintain transcripts and records of course work that has been completed.

It is advised that a portfolio or outline of topics studied be compiled by those families who are providing homeschooling independent of an accredited program or public school. To calculate credits in the United States, the general guideline is sixty hours of instruction or work in the subject area equals one semester which provides a half of a credit. To create one's own transcript the following items should be included:

- Grade level/school/school year
- Course titles
- Grades earned
- Credits earned

Although not written specifically for students with ASD, Cafi Cohen's book, *Homeschooling: The Teen Years: Your Complete Guide to Successfully Homeschooling the 13- to 18-Year-Old,* provides families with more specific detail on how to construct a homemade transcript.[4] Her Web site, www.homeschoolteenscollege.net/ hsarticles.html, provides additional information to address issues for this age group.

Some colleges will provide students with a transcript form to fill out. Contact the college that the student is interested in attending to learn if this is available. Some colleges have the forms available for downloading from their Web sites. It is always best to start researching the entrance requirements for the student's preferred colleges early so that adequate time can be given to the entire application process.

Other items that might be required for admission to college include

- Letters of recommendation from mentors, teachers, or tutors

- Personal essays stating the student's reasons for applying to the college and the selected career path

- A standardized test, which might include the General Equivalency Diploma (GED) in lieu of a high school diploma and the SAT or ACT, which are standard entrance exams that are typically taken by the student in the eleventh or twelfth grade. Students can take these tests more than once; however, the tests are only given at certain times of the year. Students should contact their local school district to find out when and where the tests will be offered. Some colleges and universities do not require SAT or ACT scores. For a list of these schools, visit the Fair Test Web site at www.fairtest.org/univ/optional.htm.

Scholarships are becoming more available to homeschooled students. As with any scholarship, students must meet the specific requirements for the scholarship. For information about home-school scholarships, check out the following Web sites www.eho

.org/hsscholarships.htm   and   www.hsadvisor.com/scholarships
.html. Information is available on financial aid and student loans
at www.finaid.org and www.fafsa.ed.gov.

The preceding paragraphs address the basics that any homeschooled high-school-aged student must do to prepare for
college. Lars Perner, Ph.D., a university professor who also has
Asperger Syndrome, encourages an early start in planning to help
keep individuals with ASD on the correct path.[5] The question to
answer now is what special accommodations or considerations
need to occur to assist the student with ASD as he prepares for college. As mentioned in Question 2, many families choose to homeschool their child with ASD because traditional school did not
meet their child's unique learning needs or the social demands
were too great. One might think that the demands of traditional
college might also be too great; however, some people with ASD
refute this thought.

Stephen Shore, an adult man with autism, states that in college
people appreciated him for who he was instead of making fun of
him for his differences. He comments that the predictability and
structure of the day helped him. The opportunity to take classes of
interest provided him great enjoyment and resulted in a double
major on graduation.[6]

Liane Holliday Willey, an adult woman with Asperger Syndrome,
states that "with a strong support system and a healthy interest in a
field of study, those with Asperger's will often find they have just
what it takes to make their college years a wonderful experience.
Where else but in college can you obsess on your interests and get
rewarded for doing so?"[7]

A counselor on a community college campus advised that the
most important knowledge and skills a student can bring to college
is a self-awareness of how his disability affects learning and how to

self-advocate to get the accommodations needed to be successful. The student should also have an understanding that there are laws and rights that protect individuals with disabilities.

This knowledge needs to be systematically taught over the many years leading up to college. Very young children can be taught about their strengths and challenges and how to ask for help. As a child matures, more details may be shared about ASD and how it affects one's life and learning. There are a variety of books that may be helpful to families as they explain ASD to their child including

- *What Does It Mean to Me? A Workbook Explaining Self Awareness and Life Lessons to the Child or Youth with High-Functioning Autism or Asperger's* (2000) by Cathrine Faherty and Gary Mesibov.
- *Finding Out About Asperger Syndrome, High Functioning Autism and PDD* (1997) by Gunilla Gerland.
- *Freaks, Geeks & Asperger Syndrome: A User Guide to Adolescence* (2002) by Luke Jackson.
- *Asperger's Huh? A Child's Perspective* (1999) by Rosina Schnurr.
- *How to Be Yourself in a World That's Different: An Asperger Syndrome Study Guide for Adolescents* (2007) by Yuko Yoshida.[8]

Helping children understand their unique qualities is not the same as labeling them in a negative way. A person with a medical condition such as diabetes needs to understand their condition to maintain good health. The same is true of a person with ASD. The person with ASD must understand their neurological differences to keep themselves healthy both socially and emotionally. When they are able to do this, they become their best as a learner, worker, and friend.

The right time to begin to discuss this with a child is dependent on several variables. Many have stated that the information should be shared as soon as the child is capable of understanding it conceptually. When children begin to express frustration, parents can explain how everyone's brain works differently. Sharing that everyone has strengths and weakness can move directly into a discussion of ASD.

Regardless of when a child learns about his disability, it is critical that he develops self-awareness so that he can advocate for himself in college, work, and the world. Following self-awareness, the child must be taught how, when, and to whom he should disclose this personal information. There are two excellent books to assist parents, educators, and adolescents or adults in gaining a greater understanding of disclosure and self-advocacy. These "must-read" books include worksheets and lesson to teach these critical skills:

- *Asperger Syndrome: An Owner's Manual for Older Adolescents and Adults: What You, Your Parents and Friends, and Your Employer, Need to Know* (2007) by Ellen S. Korin.

- *Ask and Tell: Self-Advocacy and Disclosure for People on the Autism Spectrum* (2004) by Stephen Shore, editor.[9]

When the student with ASD gets on a college campus, he will need to set up a support system on campus. Even if the student is attending a community college and living at home, he will need support on campus. For the student living away from home, either in a dorm or apartment, the support system may need to be more comprehensive and include daily living basics such as money management, cooking, cleaning, and time management, to name a few. The student coming from a homeschool background may have had many more opportunities to practice these important life skills. This is a big plus for surviving the transition from home to the real world.

Liane Holliday Willey, an adult woman with Asperger Syndrome, has outlined key support systems that one must establish to survive the college transition.[10] She suggests support systems to address social impairments such as courses in speech, communication, sociology, psychology, and dramatic arts; asking a counselor to assist in establishing friendships through clubs, peer tutoring, or mentors; and using a counselor to help select teachers who are empathetic and willing to make accommodations as needed.

Surviving the geographic issues of a college campus takes planning. If needed, the student can ask for disabled student parking, access to elevators, or even special transportation. Becoming familiar with campus landmarks by using either notes or audiotape can be helpful. Practicing finding classes or other important locations on campus, at times when few students are on the campus, is usually a good idea. Exploring the campus prior to the beginning of classes builds the confidence needed to deal with the large crowds of people present when classes are in session.

Planning, prioritizing, organization, and using time wisely are executive functioning skills that may require support. Counselors can be helpful in keeping the course load manageable and scheduled throughout the week to allow for study time and relaxation or possibly a job. Keeping a calendar is necessary to track due dates. The student should always have a support person or parents review scheduling to prevent confusion.

The student should have a survival plan for dealing with stress. This could involve planning a time for relaxation throughout the day. When becoming familiar with the campus, the student should identify places that are calming and could provide a few minutes to regroup if needed. Knowing one's own individual needs, whether it is exercise, music, or even journaling thoughts and feelings, is essential for stress management. Many of these stress-reduction strategies may not have been as necessary when homeschooling; however, in the busy world of a college campus the student may need to develop a plan to address stress.

Parent Perspective

Make an appointment for you and your child to meet with the college disabilities office to set up any needed accommodations or supports. Encourage your child to take one or two college classes while in high school, if possible, or just have the child take one or two college classes per semester to get started while you figure out what the child will need to succeed. Follow the same path as preparing for high school transition by visiting campus, meeting teachers ahead of time, and so on, in order to make a smoother transition.

—Karen Crum

If the student is receiving special education services, the IEP team should be involved in the transition process. Transition planning is required by law for any child with an IEP.

—Janelle Lewis

Planning to go to college is a big step for any individual. It requires organization, planning, and problem-solving skills. This, along with some of the same issues that prompted the original decision to homeschool, may prompt some students with ASD to look for other options that are a continuation of homeschooling at a college level. One similar option involves online or distance learning through a college or university. If online or distance learning has already been a part of the homeschool program, this will be a natural transition to opportunities at the college level. Some colleges do require students to spend some time on campus. A list of colleges and universities offering online or distance learning can be found at www.collegedegree.com. Information on accredited degree programs and certificates for specialized trainings can be found at the Distance Education and Training Council: www.detc .org. *Campus-Free College Degrees,* written by Marcie Thorson (1998), may also provide families with helpful information on obtaining a higher education while learning at home.

20 | What Are Other Postsecondary Options Besides College?

When a child has an IEP and is being served in public school, the law requires that transition goals be developed and documented in the IEP. This transition planning takes place by the age of sixteen or younger as appropriate. For the child who is privately home-schooled, the transition goals may not be formalized in an IEP; however, planning for postsecondary life should still be addressed by age sixteen. Addressing transition goals early is very important, as students with ASD may require more time and training to make the transition to the adult world. It has been reported that without guidance in developing their talents or the proper supports most individuals with ASD are unemployed and underemployed.[11]

As revealed in Question 19, many things must be accomplished prior to moving on to college and higher education. The same is true for the young adult who does not wish to seek a higher education. Employment options for those choosing not to continue their education might include competitive employment, supported employment, or self-employment.

For individuals with more significant challenges, employment may not be a goal. Families may want their young adult to be active in the community and pursue personal interests that are more appropriate to his interests or level of endurance. Some families may choose to continue to participate in the type of activities they have been doing during the homeschool years. Others may want to explore day activity centers where postsecondary-age individuals participate in various community activities or day programs based on interests such as fine arts and crafts. Some of the arts-based programs display and sell the pieces created by members of the group.

If the teen has not participated in any work experiences during his high school years and employment is a goal, he and his parents might explore volunteer work, apprenticeships, internships, or supported employment with a mentor or job coach. The Department of Vocational Rehabilitation might be a helpful resource. As with college, the young adult will need to understand the types of support he will need, and again determine how much to disclose about his disability and to whom.

Temple Grandin is a strong advocate of early work experience for children with ASD.[12] She suggests that taking responsibility for personal items and picking up after oneself are vocational skills that begin early in childhood. Behavioral, social, emotional regulation, organizational, and scheduling skills that a child learns are all foundational skills for becoming a productive citizen. Parents should continually teach the skills that develop a good work ethic from a very early age, while nurturing the child's special interests. The following scenario demonstrates how parents might infuse the skills needed to be a successful employee—as an adult—into a child's daily routine:

- Child wakes up using an alarm clock (scheduling skills)
- Child gets ready for the day by washing face, brushing teeth, and getting dressed (organizational skills and adaptive skills)
- Child greets family at breakfast table (social skills)
- Child asks for help pouring milk (self-advocacy)

- Child checks daily schedule and notices a change (emotional regulation)
- Child completes assignments and tasks (organizational skills)

Grandin suggests that the transition to work be gradual, with work hours kept short in the beginning. She encourages individuals with ASD to follow their interests and explore ways to make their special interest become their career. Freelance work that focuses on one's special interest is a perfect match for someone who does better in an environment that can be personalized to meet individual needs. Parents and educators will find much wisdom and support from Grandin's books *Thinking in Pictures, Developing Talents: Careers for Individuals with Asperger Syndrome and High-Functioning Autism.*[13]

Other resources related to adult transition that parents and educators might find helpful include

- "Marketing a Person on the Autistic Spectrum: Some Business School Lessons" (2004) by Lars Perner, www.larsperner.com.
- *Making Self-Employment Work for People with Disabilities* (2003) by Cary Griffin and David Hammis.
- *A Guide to Successful Employment for Individuals with Autism* (1995) by Marcia Smith, Ronald Belcher, and Patricia Juhrs.[14]

Whether an individual seeks employment after high school, attends college, or participates in a sheltered day program, they will still need to face challenges that will require a support system that expands beyond parents. Finding mentors that understand the unique needs of the individual with ASD and who can provide guidance through the social and communicative requirements of a job and life is critical to success as an adult. The mentors may be paid staff, coworkers, or friends.

Autism is a lifelong disability that may affect one's cognitive abilities, but always affects one's social and communicative skills. These skill deficits affect interactions and relationships at home, school, and in the workplace and must be continually supported. Planning for success and productive participation in the world requires that the following two components be achieved. First, there must be early systematic planning from a young age for interesting activities that will sustain motivation throughout adulthood; and second, there must be a network of support to meet the identified goals. Successful transitioning to the adult world requires a team and teamwork regardless of the end goal.

Questions for Homeschooling Parents

Interview with Janelle Lewis

Janelle Lewis is the mother of Ben, age eleven. Janelle has a master's degree in education with a specialization in curriculum and instruction. She holds both multiple- and single-subject credentials. She has been teaching for more than twenty years in K–9 classrooms. Her experience has been in traditional and alternative settings, including serving as a homeschool instructor for a public homeschool program. Janelle has been honored in national publications for her work in curriculum development and implementation. She volunteers on several committees related to developmental disabilities and is an active advocate for parent and student rights. Just for fun she enjoys family camping trips, organic gardening, perfecting the art of gluten-free/casein-free cooking, visits to the coast, searching for treasures among junk, identifying wildflowers, and spending time at home with her family and dogs.

When and how did you discover your child had a diagnosis on the Autism Spectrum? Ben's ASD was regressive; he has immune system issues and has suffered ongoing consequences from environmental toxins. Ben began receiving services for motor delays shortly after his first birthday. By his second birthday, he was also receiving speech therapy and occupational therapy. It was not until after his third birthday that he received his ASD diagnosis. Looking back, it was definitely a missed diagnosis that should have been made much earlier.

Describe your child's school history. Ben's school history started on a negative note with the insistence by the school officials that he be assigned to a county autism preschool program. This was not an appropriate placement, as evidenced by the emotional trauma he experienced daily in this setting and by the self-injurious behaviors that resulted. The teacher and aide in this program were not trained to work with children with ASD, and the other students had behaviors that were very disturbing to Ben. We eventually pulled him out of that program. With great effort and endurance, we were finally able to provide Ben with a quality in-home Applied Behavior Analysis (ABA) program for up to forty hours per week, which was articulated between the home and school settings.

When he had the necessary skills, Ben began attending a preschool with typical peers, accompanied by his ABA tutor and supervisor. His in-home program continued to focus on both functional/behavioral and educational goals. Ben made incredible progress with his ABA program in place, and his one-on-one home and school instructional assistants, trained and supervised by a nonpublic agency (NPA), were no longer needed by the end of second grade.

In third grade, Ben was "on his own" at school, and he did very well academically and socially; however, things changed for him in fourth grade. When he left his K–3 school for a 4–6 school, the social climate became much more complex, and Ben had a tough time understanding and keeping up. Academically, he was still able to perform at grade level; however, we still did a lot of curricular pre-teaching and follow-up at home. As his understanding of the increasingly complex social cues and emotions of peers and adults became more difficult, Ben's emotional state suffered, and he became increasingly anxious and depressed. By the end of fourth grade, we made the decision to homeschool Ben for fifth grade and to reassess what was best for him each year thereafter.

What aspects of traditional schooling worked for your child? Ben's successful early years in public school resulted from the willingness of his regular education teachers to learn about ASD and work as a team with his home program providers and with us. We were very fortunate in being able to have Ben placed, against the wishes of school administrators, in a multi-age, regular education, combination K–2 class. In this program, he had the same incredibly dedicated and talented teachers and most of the same peers with him for three years. His teachers saw him go from needing a full-time one-on-one instructional assistant as a kindergartener, to being able to succeed on his own at school by the end of second grade. The school staff worked with us through all facets of Ben's ABA program as it was implemented at school. That multi-age setting had a warm, relaxed family feel to it with the older kids acting as role models and helpers for the younger kids. Most of Ben's classroom peers were part of his in-home, after-school, peer-play ABA therapy groups, and skills learned at home in those "play" sessions carried over to his social successes at this school. The parents of his multi-age peers were enthusiastic about having their children participate in Ben's after-school play/therapy groups, and they too were integral in making this home-school-NPA collaboration succeed. This model worked for Ben because we had quality ABA experts working with the classroom teachers, his peers and their families, and our family to provide an individualized program designed to meet Ben's unique needs. It should be noted that it took filing for due process and fighting many battles with public service agencies and school officials in order to get this successful program implemented, and then total dedication, much stress, and often exhaustion to keep it going. But, we would do it again in a heartbeat.

What was not effective or not working in the traditional school setting? By fourth grade, Ben amazed everyone with his academic gains, and he had a few really good buddies at school. He appeared to be a "best outcome" child with ASD. On the flip side, he worked so hard at being compliant, tuning out the sensory overload that overwhelmed him, getting the right answers, and trying to keep up socially, that he was absolutely exhausted by the time he got home from school. He had no energy for outside activities, and it was impossible to tackle homework. We decided to do the homework in the morning, before school, when he was rested. He would often fall apart and be an emotional mess as he unwound from the school day. As the year progressed, his self-esteem was shot, and he was feeling as though no one liked him anymore. Ben began to isolate himself on the playground, as understanding his peers and their changing social world became more of a mystery to him. Even though goals relating to social skills were a part of Ben's IEP, an effective program was not implemented at this time. We had come so far, but unaddressed social cognition issues were making it impossible for Ben to continue to have a positive school experience.

Ben also suffered nutritionally when attending school. While homeschooling, we discovered that he feels better and stays more focused on school work if he eats lots of small, nutritious meals throughout the day. He now tells me that he used to think about food all day long when he was at school. Even if we were to allow Ben to eat healthy snacks all day at school, he still would not want to do so unless the other kids were doing the same thing at the same time. Whether it is food, curriculum, or activities, he does not want to stand out. As part of his homeschool days, Ben has learned to plan, shop for, and prepare his meals; consequently, he is eating a much wider variety of healthy foods.

Many sensory issues still plague Ben, and the school setting was filled with aversive sounds, flickering lights, and annoying smells. It was very difficult for him to concentrate under those circumstances.

How did you learn about or discover homeschooling as an option? I am a credentialed public school teacher with a master's degree in curriculum and instruction, but I knew next-to-nothing about homeschooling as an option until I was actually hired to teach in a county home study program. After Ben entered kindergarten, I was fortunate to be hired part-time to teach in a public school "alternative" home study program, where I had much flexibility in my schedule and could adjust it to meet my family's needs. I spent five years teaching in that program, and during that time, I worked with many families and learned about the varied reasons they choose homeschooling and about the many program options available to them. Homeschooling, even with the public education options now available, is still a mystery to many educational professionals. I was lucky to have learned about homeschooling firsthand as a teacher working with homeschooling families.

Interview with Karen Crum

Karen Crum is the parent of fifteen-year-old Katie, a sophomore. Karen has a doctoral degree in public health and preventive care. In 2002, she founded Successful Living with Autism through Training and Education (S.L.A.T.E.), which provides after-school and summer social-emotional training to children with autism, as well as parent and community training. She is an active member of her church, and serves on the board of the Autism Society of Northern California and on an advisory council for the Shasta County Mental Health Board. Dr. Crum speaks to diverse groups on topics related to autism, parenting children with special needs, faith, and coping with grief. In her spare time, she enjoys the family pets, reading, gardening, acting in community theatre, and spending time with her wonderful husband and two beautiful teenage daughters.

"When and how did you discover your child had a diagnosis on the Autism Spectrum?" Katie was showing symptoms starting at about eighteen months to two years of age that were becoming noticeable to me, the mother. Few others could see it, and she was labeled as having an anxiety disorder for at least a year. I suspected high-functioning autism soon after this diagnosis, knowing there were other symptoms that fit. She finally received an official diagnosis of mild autism at age three-and-a-half.

Describe your child's school history. Katie attended traditional private preschools, which had smaller classroom sizes compared to public classrooms. She also received consultation from special educators and a privately hired autism specialist. As parents, we provided at-home social-emotional training using college students we hired and trained when Katie was age three-and-a-half to age five-and-a-half. Katie attended a highly structured private Christian school from kindergarten through fifth grade, with few or no classroom supports, and did quite well in this setup until sixth grade. During the course of her early education, she received Occupational Therapy (OT), speech therapy, "Fun Club" (an after-school social training group), lots of home-directed social and speech training, and planned home "social summer school."

What about traditional schooling worked for your child? The highly structured environment at the private Christian school was good for Katie. Assignments were very predictable and clear. People were generally kind and helpful to her in the elementary grades, and she had a few wonderfully enthusiastic teachers who helped her laugh and learn at the same time. Katie learned how to play basketball and kickball, and she participated in some wonderful musical and drama presentations with her classes.

What was not effective or working in the traditional school setting? By the end of fifth grade and the beginning of sixth, both the social and academic expectations became more than Katie could bear, and she became very anxious. Hiring an experienced classroom aide was not adequate because Katie was very aware of needing help, especially in math, and she felt stupid that she needed the help. First we tried a half day of homeschool with Katie attending the traditional school in the morning. Then, as the sixth graders became more self-centered, a few key people important to Katie began to be unkind. By October of sixth grade, she was crying herself to sleep four nights a week and her self-esteem had plummeted. It was no longer a very positive or effective environment in which to learn or socialize, and I did not feel that switching to a public school at that point would offer her much help.

How did you learn about or discover homeschooling as an option? I guess I always knew it was an option for *someone,* but never considered *I* would do it. However, a good friend from another state had recently moved to the same town as our family, and she had been homeschooling for about four years. I trusted her as a reasonable, nonradical type of person and began to ask her about homeschooling. She encouraged me that I could do it. Also, Katie's school aide and program specialist thought it was a reasonable and good option. I prayed about it and researched it. I found a local charter school, which allowed Katie to attend classes two mornings a week in addition to school at home. This seemed doable to me, as I perceived that both Katie and I needed social contact away from one another at least a few mornings a week.

Interview with Connie Ajay

Connie Ajay is the parent of Bobby, age thirteen. In addition to her very important role of Mom, she is an active member of the Families for Early Autism Treatment (FEAT), as well as a parent mentor and trainer. She is also an active member of her school district's Community Advisory Committee (CAC). Connie and her husband own a karate school, where they provide instruction to students of all abilities. She coauthored a checklist for parents of newly diagnosed children entitled *Autism Spectrum Disorder (ASD): So You Have a Diagnosis, Now What?*[1] Just for fun, Connie loves to go to Disneyland.

"When and how did you discover your child had a diagnosis on the Autism Spectrum?" He was not fully diagnosed until he was four, because of the lack of understanding of ASD in higher-functioning children back in the early to late 1990s.

"Describe your child's school history." My son started with preschool and early intervention at the age of four. He was placed in a speech-delayed class for kindergarten and was not offered any services due to my lack of understanding of the system. As I discovered his rights, he was enrolled in first grade in a full inclusion program with an aide. He received Extended School Year (ESY), Resource Specialist (RSP), Speech Therapy, and Occupational Therapy (OT) his entire time during his elementary school years. We transferred to homeschooling during seventh grade (middle school), where he continues to receive speech, OT, and RSP services through the charter school.

"What aspects of traditional schooling worked for your child?" During his time in public elementary school, it was easier to navigate with one teacher. The other children were his main source of social opportunities, and they were accepting of him and provided a wealth of support.

"What was not effective or not working in the traditional school setting?" The educators working with him lacked the understanding of ASD, specifically the executive functioning and the sensory integration components and how they manifested in his educational day.

"*How did you learn about or discover homeschooling as an option?*" I knew about homeschooling; however, I did my own research to see if it was an option for my son. I was confirmed in my decision when I heard Tony Attwood, a world renowned expert in ASD, speak about the middle-school years.

Interview with Michelle King

Michelle King is the parent of sixth grader Justin. Michelle has had varied interests in her life; however, her current single focus is her family. Growing up, Michelle was a tournament water skier. Throughout school she loved all sports and enjoyed her Spanish classes. After getting married, her husband asked her what she wanted to be; Michelle replied, "I want to be a mommy." She and her husband have two boys. When her boys were in elementary school, she worked as a librarian. This is a job that Michelle cherishes to this day. Michelle states, "I will have my time for a job later in life; for right now, my family is everything."

"*When and how did you discover your child had a diagnosis on the Autism Spectrum?*" In preschool his teacher said there was something not right. After that, every year the teachers said the same thing. Starting with first grade the teachers wanted Justin tested. In the spring of second grade, we finally were referred to a child psychologist who gave no clear diagnosis. Justin began receiving limited speech therapy. I held Justin back in third grade. This is when we realized that the school wasn't willing to help us; they actually said that, so we moved to our current community and began homeschooling. Justin returned to public school in the spring of his second round of third grade. In the fall of fourth grade, a psychologist with the State Diagnostic Center finally diagnosed Justin as having high-functioning autism.

"Describe your child's school history." Justin went to a private pre-school and public elementary. He went to summer school after his first year of third grade and then was retained in the third grade again. Justin received some speech/language; however, to be very honest the teacher gave me the work and handed me a book and asked me to pick his lessons. That's when I knew it was time to move on. He was homeschooled again in the winter/spring of third grade, then moved back to a mainstream third-grade class. He continues to remain in the same district now in sixth grade at the middle school.

"What about traditional schooling worked for your child?" Justin adored every teacher he had. It wasn't until we moved to our current community that he received an incredible amount of special education support from aides, a speech/language therapist, resource specialists (RST), and his teachers.

"What was not effective or not working in the traditional school setting?" It seemed that no one was trained to adapt to the needs of Justin even after we began the process of diagnosis. This was until we moved to our current community.

"How did you learn about or discover homeschooling as an option?" I felt there were no other options and that if we wanted Justin to feel successful and gain some self-esteem, one-on-one education was best. I felt that there was no other choice.

Interview with Ann Coe

Ann Coe is the parent of Ian, age seventeen. Ann is a graduate of the University of California, Davis. She is a small animal veterinarian. She reduced her practice to weekends when the decision was made to homeschool her son. Currently she only works on weekends. Her interest in animals influences her community service activities. She volunteers at the local Natural Science Museum and also takes the

Zoo-mobile to school classrooms, where she does presentations on various animals. She supports other families who have children with disabilities by running a small parent support group through the Family Empowerment Center. She enjoys many outside activities with her family including skiing, backpacking, and biking.

"When and how did you discover your child had a diagnosis on the Autism Spectrum?" At nine years old, my son was diagnosed with ADHD and anxiety by a private psychologist. My sister, who is also a psychologist, suggested that we read an article on Asperger's. A local psychiatrist agreed with this diagnosis. Ian didn't have a formal diagnostic assessment using the Autism Diagnostic Observation Schedule (ADOS) until he was seventeen years old. Then he was classified as High Functioning Autistic (HFA).

"Describe your child's school history." We held Ian back one year before starting kindergarten. He has attended regular classes at public school from kindergarten through eighth grade. He has had private speech therapy since two years of age because of his cleft lip and palate and later through the school because of his poor social skills. In sixth through eighth grades, he had a 504 Plan and got some resource help in math and a little occupational therapy. He also went to a private tutor for math after school during seventh grade. We sent him to a small weekly group psychology session for about six months. He has attended "G.E.T. S.E.T," a social-emotional skills training group for children with ASD, every summer for about five years. In high school he has an IEP. We spent from one to three hours every evening from second though eighth grades helping him with school work after a full day of schooling. This generally included weekends and vacations too.

"What aspects of traditional schooling worked for your child?" The routine of traditional school was good for Ian. The teachers tried to accommodate him. He felt like part of a group. The other kids helped him stay tuned in some of the time. He was considered

"smart" because of his interest in academic subjects and his great vocabulary. The other kids thought he was funny because he always said what they were thinking but wouldn't say, such as, "This class is really boring" or "She has a booger stuck to her nose." He was invited to a lot of parties in elementary school.

"What was not effective or not working in the traditional school setting?" Ian didn't get much work done in class. He spent a lot of time not listening and not being on the right page. He was often stressed out and very distracted by every noise, light, smell, and texture that he encountered. He had some negative experiences with other kids, like being rejected or teased. He didn't want to participate in P.E. in sixth through eighth grades, and was sometimes allowed to wander in the school yard and pick at the concrete wall. He couldn't relate what was happening at school to us at home. He didn't know when assignments were due, what was expected, or what was important to learn. He didn't bring home the right materials. He didn't eat enough at school. There was a lag period between doing the work and finding out if it was done right. He had to spend time on things that he already knew and didn't have enough time for things that were a challenge for him. One great example of this was when I had to drag him away from a computer visualization of Einstein's theory of relativity so he could copy his spelling words three times, even though he already knew how to spell those words.

"How did you learn about or discover homeschooling as an option?" I knew a couple of mothers who homeschooled their kids with ASD. They understood the amount of time we were spending after school catching up on class work and doing homework. There was no time left to teach Ian to do chores or to work on life skills. Since I had been very involved in Ian's schooling since preschool, it was a small step to homeschooling. I had already done eighth-grade

math, science, English, and history with him. As a parent, it is very stressful and time consuming talking to teachers just to make sure your child is doing the right work, not to mention dealing appropriately with behavioral issues. Sometimes it is easier just to do school at home. I checked on a couple of charter homeschool programs in my area and chose the program that was the best match for us.

7

Questions for Homeschooled Children on the Autism Spectrum

Interview with Ben—Age Eleven

"Tell us a little about yourself." My name is Ben Joseph Lewis. I just turned eleven years old, and I am in fifth grade. I really like dogs. I have a yellow lab named Maggie and a black lab named Proper. I love them both very much, and I get to spend lots of time with them when I am homeschooling. They know that when my timer goes off we get to go outside together for recess. We play a lot of fetch and hide-and-seek. Proper is allowed to go with us on community outings and field trips, because she is my Skilled Companion dog from Canine Companions for Independence. She wears a special vest so that people know she is allowed in public places. I have my own Doggie Day Care business, and I take care of at least two other dogs every week. I also like video games, movies, drawing, using my imagination, reading, dancing, riding horses,

213

Figure 7.1.   Ben Joseph Lewis. Ben loves his dogs.

and ice skating. I do not like mean people and seafood—except for lobster from Maine and crab from Alaska.

"How long have you been in homeschooling?" I have been homeschooling for almost six months.

"How has homeschooling helped you?" I think that homeschooling has made me smarter and happier. It has helped me to think more about me and what I like to do. I also get to spend more time with my mom and dad and my dogs.

"In what ways was traditional school hard for you?" Traditional school was hard for me in some ways. Doing art and making friends were two hard things. People talked too much on the bus, and that really bothered me. At school, I felt weird like I wasn't cool, but now I know that I am okay. I now know that being unique is a good thing.

"In what ways was traditional school easy for you?" Traditional school was easy for me when we did spelling and math. I was one of the smartest kids in spelling and math.

"In what ways is homeschooling better than traditional school?" Homeschooling is better than traditional school, because I have

lots of time to do activities like be a teacher's aide at my old school in the multi-age class. I like helping the younger kids and being with my old teachers. When I am homeschooling, I get to go lots of places with my mom. I like being with her all day.

"Is there anything you miss about traditional school?" What I miss about traditional school is six friends, but I still get to see some of them now. I have also met some new homeschooling friends.

"Do you think homeschooling is preparing you for your life as an adult? How?" I do think that homeschooling is preparing me for life as an adult. I know how to have a job and money, because I have my Doggie Day Care business. I know a lot more about food, and I am way healthier. I also know how to do lots of chores in the house and in the garden. This will help me when I am an adult.

"Do you have any words of advice for others who may be considering homeschooling?" If other kids wanted to know about homeschooling, I would tell them that sometimes it is a lot like regular school, but you might be sitting at the kitchen table or on the couch. You will still be doing work and learning, but sometimes it can even be in your pajamas. You get to do some really interesting things. If you want to try it, it can be lots of fun.

Interview with Bobby—Age Thirteen

"Tell us a little about yourself." My name is Bobby Ajay. I am thirteen, almost fourteen. I am in the eighth grade, and I go to a Charter School Homeschool. I like reading, writing stories, and doing drama. I love to be in plays and skits. I want to be a children's author when I graduate school. I dislike swimming because I don't like to put my head in the water and I don't like getting wet. I like music, especially "Old School." My Ipod is filled with Old School music. I *absolutely love* Disneyland. My ultimate dream is to live there. I know pretty much all there is to know about Disneyland.

Figure 7.2.   Bobby Ajay: Here is Bobbie with Goofy at his favorite place on earth.

"How long have you been in homeschooling?" I have done homeschooling ever since I was in the seventh grade. Before that I went to public school.

"How has homeschooling helped you?" Homeschooling has helped me because I can learn by myself. I don't have to deal with kids who are obnoxious. Also, when I have a question or problem I don't have to wait to ask my question, and sometimes my Mom knows when I don't understand by the look on my face. Plus, I don't have to listen to the teacher's blah, blah, blah. It sounds like Charlie Brown's teacher talking when the teachers talk too much. This makes me feel like my head is going to explode.

"In what ways was traditional school hard for you?" Traditional school was hard because of all the extra blah, blah, blah around me. Also, there were too many directions. I didn't know where to go and what I needed to do. This made me feel discouraged, and I just wanted to give up. Sometimes I needed to take a break and

they would not let me. This made me feel upset and really overwhelmed. They just didn't understand.

"*In what ways was traditional school easy for you?*" Traditional school was easy in the subjects of reading and spelling. I liked it when the teacher called on me to read the story because she would compliment me on how I read the story with great voices and energy.

"*In what ways is homeschooling better than traditional school?*" Homeschooling is better because I don't have to do homework because my Mom knows what I need to work on. I can also take breaks whenever I need them so I don't get overstimulated. Plus, I can take karate for my P.E. during the day when the classes are small. My Mom doesn't make me do yucky long projects either. This makes me feel like my head is going to explode.

"*Is there anything you miss about traditional school?*" I don't really miss anything except the playground, but my Mom told me I don't get playgrounds at middle school, so I would not have missed middle school. It was fun to play outside so I can get my exercise and my brain can work again. I do miss my friends though, 'cause I don't get to see them every day.

"*Do you think homeschooling is preparing you for your life as an adult? How?*" Homeschooling is getting me ready for grown-up life because I feel like it is a business and I am going to work. Also, my Mom teaches me about buying groceries, making change, and other things they don't teach you in regular school.

"*Do you have any words of advice for others who may be considering homeschooling?*" I would tell others who are thinking about homeschooling that they must have a Mom who is patient and loving because you spend a lot of time together. I love my Mom, so it doesn't bother me. She is cool and pretty. If they do like their Mom then they should do it because no one can teach you better than your Mom 'cause she wants you to do your best.

An Interview with Katie—Age Fifteen

"Tell us a little about yourself." My name is Katie Crum. I am fifteen years old, and I am in tenth grade. I like animals, sports, horseback riding, video games, reading, and hanging out with my friends. I don't like fast, twisting roller coasters, long classes, very loud places, or my sister (sometimes).

"How long have you done homeschooling?" I have been home-schooled since the sixth grade.

"How has homeschooling helped you?" I can work at my own pace, and I don't feel so stressed out.

Figure 7.3. Katie Crum: Katie with her favorite fat kitty.

"In what ways was traditional school hard for you?" Making friends and understanding hard work assignments.

"In what ways was traditional school easy for you?" Traditional school was never really easy for me, although I was good at reading and spelling.

"In what ways is homeschooling better than traditional school?" I can work at my own pace, and I have more control over what I want to work on.

"Is there anything you miss about traditional school?" I do miss being with my friends all day, and sometimes wish that I wasn't homeschooled for that reason.

"Do you think homeschooling is preparing you for your life as an adult? How?" Yes. I have learned how to do things like laundry and other chores earlier than I might have if I were in traditional school.

"Do you have any words of advice for others who may be considering homeschooling?" Homeschooling is a good thing to try if traditional school is stressful or difficult.

Interview with Ian—Age Seventeen

"Tell us a little about yourself." My name is Ian Coe. I am seventeen years old, and I am in eleventh grade. I like video games, science, reading, news updates on current events, volcanic eruptions, and learning about the Avian Flu. I don't like people that are more talkative than me, tomatoes, litter, James Bond, and other excessively violent movies.

"How long have you done homeschooling?" I have been homeschooled for two-and-a-half years.

"How has homeschooling helped you?" Homeschooling is an environment where I can adapt by moving to another room in the house if one room gets too distracting. I can learn at my own pace. I have more of the day to get work done.

Figure 7.4. Ian Coe. Ian on a family campout at Haleakala Crater.

"In what ways was traditional school hard for you?" In a traditional school, I was stuck in one environment. I got bored easily. Other people were the biggest distractions. My classmates at the home-school are better behaved than the kids in my eighth grade class.

"In what ways was traditional school easy for you?" Traditional school was not easier.

"In what ways is homeschooling better than traditional school?" At the homeschool facility, the staff understands my disabilities.

"Is there anything you miss about traditional school?" I made lots of friends there. I miss that.

"Do you think homeschooling is preparing you for your life as an adult? How?" Homeschooling is preparing me for life as an adult. I'm getting to the point where I have to control what my mind is focused on. I can stay focused on work for a longer time than I used to. It's helping me get ready for college. It's teaching me stuff that I need for college like Chemistry.

"Do you have any words of advice for others who may be considering homeschooling?" In order to apply yourself to your work, you need to apply your mind first. You must control impulses that don't have to do with work and suppress them as long as you can so you get your work done. If you can't focus any longer, you should switch to another subject so you can keep working. If stress continues long enough that you realize that you have problems with traditional school, then get some information about different homeschools to figure out if homeschool has advantages. If you take some classes in the homeschool facility, then you have a better chance of being able to get things done in traditional school. It will help you adapt to the regular classroom so you don't lose the experience of a traditional classroom.

GLOSSARY OF TERMS AND ACRONYMS

ABA: Applied Behavior Analysis is the science of applying experimentally derived principles of behavior to improve socially significant behavior. ABA takes what we know about behavior and uses it to bring about positive change (Applied). Behaviors are defined in observable and measurable terms in order to assess change over time (Behavior). The behavior is analyzed within the environment to determine what factors are influencing the behavior (Analysis).

Accommodation is an *adjustment* that allows a student to complete the same assignment or test as the other students, but with a change in the timing, formatting, setting, scheduling, response, and/or presentation. An accommodation does not alter in any significant way what the test or assignment measures.

Autistic Disorder is sometimes referred to as *early infantile autism* or *childhood autism*. Children with Autistic Disorder have a moderate to severe range of difficulties in the areas of both verbal and nonverbal communication; reciprocal socialization; and restricted routines, rituals, and patterns of behavior. Many resources indicate that approximately 70 percent of children with autism also have cognitive delays. This disorder is four times more common in boys than in girls.

Autistic-Like Behavior is a term used to describe students in educational settings as part of the process of qualifying for special education. To be eligible for special education, a student must present with one of thirteen qualifying disabilities and have deficits that impact their ability to achieve educational benefit without additional supports and services. Code of Federal Regulations 1308.15 describes the educational disability of Autism as a developmental disability significantly affecting verbal and nonverbal communication and social interaction generally evident prior to age three that adversely affects the child's educational performance. Other characteristics often associated with autism are engagement in repetitive activities and stereotyped movements, resistance to environmental change or change in daily routines, and unusual responses to sensory experiences. The term does not apply if the child's educational performance is adversely affected primarily because the child has an emotional disturbance, as defined in 300.7(b)(4). Each state has it's own set of supplemental regulations, which may vary from this definition somewhat.

ADD/ADHD: Attention Deficit Disorder/Attention Deficit with Hyperactivity Disorder are neurobehavioral disorders that are characterized by a persistent pattern of inattention and/or hyperactivity (hyperactive type), as well as forgetfulness, poor impulse control or impulsivity, and distractibility. This disability affects approximately 3–5 percent of school-aged children and typically presents symptoms in childhood. ADD/ADHD is currently considered to be a persistent and chronic condition for which no medical cure is available, although medication can be prescribed. ADD/ADHD is most commonly diagnosed in children and, over the past decade, has been increasingly diagnosed in adults. About 60 percent of children diagnosed with ADHD retain the condition as adults. It appears to be highly heritable, although one-fifth of all cases are estimated to be caused from trauma or toxic exposure. Methods of treatment usually involve some combination of medications, behavior modifications, lifestyle changes, and counseling.

AS: Asperger Syndrome is named after Austrian pediatrician Hans Asperger who, in 1944, identified a set of unique social and behavioral characteristics in a group of children. Today AS is one of several Autism Spectrum Disorders (ASD), which are characterized by difficulties in social interaction and by restricted, stereotyped patterns of behavior, interests and activities. AS differs from other Autism Spectrum Disorders in two ways. Those diagnosed with AS meet the early milestones for language development and have normal to above-normal cognitive abilities. Although not mentioned in standard diagnostic criteria, motor clumsiness and atypical use of language are frequently reported.

ASD: Autism Spectrum Disorder is the term used to describe a group of neurobiological Pervasive Developmental Disorders (PDD) that are characterized by specific impairments in social interaction and communication, and cause restricted and repetitive patterns of behavior. The diagnostic labels of ASD range from the milder Asperger Syndrome (AS) and Pervasive Developmental Disorder–Not Otherwise Specified (PDD-NOS) to moderate Autistic Disorder and the more severe Autistic Disorder with coexisting mental retardation, seizures, and other disorders.

CD: Conduct Disorder is a psychiatric condition described in the DSM-IV as a pattern of repetitive and persistent behaviors that interfere with the rights of others or violate the current age-appropriate social norms. Symptoms include verbal and physical aggression, cruel behavior toward people and pets, destructive behavior, lying, truancy, vandalism, and stealing. After the age of eighteen, a conduct disorder may develop into antisocial personality disorder.

Childhood Disintegrative Disorder is an extremely rare disorder currently listed under the DSM-IV category of Pervasive

Developmental Disorders. In CDD, there is a clearly apparent regression in multiple areas of functioning such as the ability to move, bladder and bowel control, and social and language skills following a period of at least two years of apparently normal development. According to the American Psychiatric Association, by definition, Childhood Disintegrative Disorder can *only* be diagnosed if the symptoms are preceded by *at least* two years of normal development and the onset of decline is prior to age ten.

Cortisol Hyper-Secretion Glucocorticoids (primarily cortisol) are important metabolic hormones that help the body resist stressors by increasing blood glucose, fatty acid and amino acid levels, and blood pressure. High levels of glucocorticoids depress the immune system and the inflammatory response. ACTH is the major stimulus for glucocorticoid release.

DIS: Designated Instructional Services, sometimes called Related Services, are supplementary services provided to students that are related to their identified disability and are available when they are necessary for the student to benefit educationally from his or her instructional program. A child must qualify for an IEP before qualification for DIS is determined. DIS include, but are not limited to, speech and language development and remediation, audiological services, orientation and mobility instruction, instruction in the home or hospital, adapted physical education, physical and occupational therapy, vision therapy, specialized driver training instruction, counseling and guidance, social skills training, organizational skills training, psychological services other than assessment and development of IEP, parent counseling and training, health and nursing services, social worker services, vocational education and career development, recreation services, and specialized services for low-incidence disabilities, such as readers, transcribers, and vision and hearing services.

DTT: Discrete Trial Teaching is a primary teaching method used in teaching children with autism that was popularized following the Ivar Lovaas study publishing in 1987. The term Discrete Trial Teaching (DTT) is often synonymous with Applied Behavior Analysis (ABA), however, DTT is only one application drawn from ABA principles. A discrete trial is a single cycle of a behaviorally based instructional sequence consisting of an (Sd) instruction, (R) response, and a consequence (either a reinforcer, or corrective feedback).

Dysregulation is a term used to refer to a response that is poorly modulated and does not fall within the conventionally accepted range of responses to the current stimulus/environmental situation.

Echolalia is the repetition of vocalizations made by another person. Echolalia can be present in ASD and other developmental disabilities. The repetitious vocalization can be immediate or delayed. When done involuntarily, it is often considered a form of tic.

ED, SED, or EBD: Emotionally Disturbed, Seriously Emotionally Disturbed, or Emotional and Behavioral Disorders are broad categories that are used commonly in educational settings and described in Education Codes. These terms are used to describe children or adolescents who, based on specific behavioral criteria, are found eligible for special education supports or services. The DSM-IVR identifies many different emotional or mental disorders that may affect children or adults. Public schools do not diagnose a specific emotional or mental disorder; rather, they use the Education Code descriptions as part of the process of qualifying a child for special education.

EF: Executive Functions are a set of cognitive processes thought to be involved in activities such as planning, cognitive flexibility, abstract thinking, acquisition of rules, initiating appropriate actions, inhibiting inappropriate actions, and selecting relevant sensory information. The primary region of the brain thought to be responsible for the executive functions is the frontal cortex. Many of the activities of EF are shown to be impaired in individuals with disabilities including ASD and ADD/ADHD.

Extinction is the decline of a behavior or learned response when it is no longer followed by a reinforcer. Oftentimes there will be a temporary surge in the learned behavior (referred to as the *extinction burst)* prior to the decline in the behavior (*extinction).*

FAPE: Free and Appropriate Public Education is an educational right of disabled children in the United States that is guaranteed by IDEA. FAPE is defined as an educational program that is individualized to a specific child, is designed to meet that child's unique needs, provides access to the general curriculum, meets the grade-level standards established by the state, and from which the child receives educational benefit. To provide FAPE to a child with a disability, schools must provide students with an education, including specialized instruction and related services, that prepares the child for further education, employment, and independent living.

FBA: Functional Behavior Assessment is generally considered to be a problem-solving process for addressing student problem behavior. Several techniques and strategies are used to identify the purposes of specific behavior, including descriptive analysis of the common triggers and consequences/outcomes and observations in the natural settings. This information helps IEP teams to select interventions that directly address the problem behavior. Functional behavioral assessment should be integrated, as appropriate, throughout the process of developing, reviewing, and if necessary, revising a student's IEP.

fMRI: functional Magnetic Resonance Imaging is a type of specialized MRI scan. It is one of the most recently developed forms of neuroimaging. Since the early 1990s, fMRI has come to dominate the brain-mapping field because of its low invasiveness, lack of radiation exposure, and relatively wide availability. Using functional magnetic resonance imaging technology (fMRI), researchers examining children with autism have discovered less activation in the deep parts of the brain responsible for certain cognitive processes such as executive function (attention, reasoning, and problem solving). Neuroimaging research is showing the dysfunction in the brain that accounts for why children with autism have problems with certain cognitive processes. Discovering neurologically why children with autism learn and organize their thoughts may help develop better interventions.

Generalization is the ability of the student to demonstrate learned skills and behaviors in conditions that vary from the original learning situation along one or more dimensions. These dimensions can include variations in the instructions, setting, materials, people, and time of day.

Graphic Organizers are visual representations of knowledge, concepts, or ideas. They are known to help relieve learner boredom, enhance recall, provide motivation, create interest, clarify information, assist in organizing thoughts, and promote understanding. Because they are a visual strategy, they are highly effective for teaching academic and social skills to children with ASD.

HFA: High Functioning Autism is a term often used to describe an individual who meets all the criteria for Autistic Disorder by thirty-six months of age, but also has average cognition and develops language skills to allow for successful functioning. Although the term HFA is frequently used by parents and professionals, it is not a diagnostic category in the DSM-IVR and therefore should be used with caution.

IDEA: Individuals with Disabilities Education Act is a United States federal law that governs how states and public agencies provide early intervention, special education, and related services to children with disabilities. It addresses the educational needs of children with disabilities from birth to the age of twenty-one.

IEP: Individual Educational Program is mandated by the Individuals with Disabilities Education Act (IDEA) in the United States. In Canada and the United Kingdom, an equivalent document is called an Individual Education Plan. Every student with a disability who is found to meet the federal and state requirements for special education must have an IEP that offers a Free Appropriate Public Education (FAPE) in the Least Restrictive Environment (LRE). The IEP refers both to the educational program to be provided to a child with a disability and to the written document that describes that educational program.

The "Individualized Educational Plan" or IEP includes present levels of student achievement and how the disability affects the student's learning; special factors that may influence learning; goals and objectives based on assessed needs; determination of the least restrictive environment for goals to be instructed; and what accommodations, modifications, and related services are required.

Independent Study is a form of education offered by many schools, colleges, and other educational institutions around the world. Sometimes it is referred to as *directed study*. Usually a student and a teacher agree on a topic for the student to further research outside of the traditional school setting with loose guidance from the instructor for an agreed-on number of credits. Many education agencies offer independent study for part or all of the curricular requirements. Homeschooling is one method of delivering independent study programs.

ISP: Individual Service Plan is a plan that offers limited consultation services to the parent or private school staff when a child with an IEP is parentally placed in a private school, including private or parochial homeschool programs. These children have no individual entitlement to special education services or funding. The ISP is different from an IEP. The services offered by and through the ISP are based on a funding formula using a proportionate amount of federal funds available to serve parentally placed private school children with disabilities under Federal Code Section 612(a)(10).

LEA: Local Education Agency refers to the school district or County Office of Education that provides the public school services in the area of residence.

Learning Style is the method of input observed to be most favored or effective for the individual student. The idea of individualized "learning styles" originated in the 1970s. It has been proposed that teachers should assess the learning styles of their students and adapt their classroom methods to best fit each student's learning style. Some of the commonly cited learning styles include visual, auditory, and tactile/kinesthetic. Most researchers believe that individuals with ASD are predominantly visual learners.

LRE: Least Restrictive Environment is identified as one of the six principles that govern the education of students with disabilities in the United States. By law, schools are required to provide a Free Appropriate Public Education (FAPE) in the least restrictive environment for students who have disabilities. LRE means that a student who has a disability should have the opportunity to be educated with nondisabled peers, to the greatest extent possible. They should have access to the general education curriculum, extracurricular activities, or any other programs that nondisabled peers would be able to access. Services and supports to help the individual to participate fully and benefit from the educational program should be determined by the IEP team. There is no single definition of what the LRE will be for each individual. It is an individual decision determined by the IEP team based on the assessed needs of the student.

Modification is an adjustment to an assignment or a test that changes the standard or what the test or assignment is supposed to measure. It does lower the difficulty or instructional level of the skill and can often be an alternative assignment or curriculum from that of same-aged peers.

MRI: Magnetic Resonance Imaging is a diagnostic procedure that uses a combination of a large magnet, radio frequencies, and a computer to produce detailed images of organs and structures within the body. An MRI is often used to examine the organs and soft tissues, to assess blood flow, to detect tumors and diagnose many forms of cancer, to evaluate infections, and to assess injuries to bones and joints. The most consistent MRI finding in autism is that the brain is enlarged. Studies have suggested that brain overgrowth may be most robust early in development, but increased brain volume has been observed throughout adolescence and early adult life.

NPA: Nonpublic Agency is a state-approved agency designed to provide special education and related services in the least restrictive environment (LRE) through the IEP process when a student's special education needs cannot be met within a given school district. A school district may contract with in-state or out-of-state NPAs.

NPS: Nonpublic School is a privately operated, publicly funded school that specializes in providing educational services for students with needs so exceptional that they cannot be met in a public school setting. In order for a child to be educated in a nonpublic school, the IEP team must determine that the public school system cannot provide the student with the instruction and services necessary to meet his or her educational needs and must identify a nonpublic school with the necessary resources and capabilities.

OCD: Obsessive Compulsive Disorder is a neuropsychiatric anxiety disorder that is characterized by recurrent, unwanted thoughts (obsessions) and/or repetitive behaviors or "rituals" (compulsions).

Common repetitive behaviors might include hand washing, counting, checking, or cleaning. These behaviors are often performed
with the hope of preventing obsessive thoughts or making them go
away. However, performing the ritual usually provides only temporary relief, and not performing it markedly increases anxiety. The
difference between OCD and the restricted interests observed with
an individual with ASD is that the person with ASD typically gains
comfort and pleasure from their routines and interests, as opposed
to discomfort and a desire to eliminate them. However, OCD can
co-occur with any of the ASDs.

ODD: Oppositional Defiant Disorder in children is an ongoing
pattern of uncooperative, defiant, and hostile behavior toward
authority figures that seriously interferes with the child's day-to-day
functioning both at home and at school. Behaviors frequently
observed in individuals with ODD may include frequent temper
tantrums, excessive arguing with adults, active defiance and refusal
to comply with adult requests and rules, deliberate attempts to
annoy or upset people, blaming others for his or her mistakes or
misbehavior, often being touchy or easily annoyed by others, frequent anger and resentment, mean and hateful talking when upset,
and seeking revenge. To meet DSM-IVR criteria, the defiance must
interfere with the child's ability to function in school, home, or the
community; cannot be the result of another disorder, such as
depression, anxiety, or the more serious conduct disorder; and must
have been happening for at least six months.

OT: Occupational Therapy can be defined simply as an activity
analysis to develop a skilled treatment plan that helps children and
adults achieve a healthy and independent lifestyle and participate
to their potential in the daily occupations of life. An occupational therapist working with an individual with ASD might develop a therapy
plan to address basic skills in handwriting, shirt buttoning, shoe tying,

or difficulty processing information through the senses. They may also work on play skills, social skills, and more.

PBSP: Positive Behavior Support Plan is a written plan developed by a team comprised of members who have personal knowledge of the individual who is communicating with behaviors that impede his or her learning or the learning of other students. Most school districts have specific forms for developing a PBSP. The plan focuses on the function (communicative intent) of the behavior with strategies identified to teach a replacement behavior that serves the same function. This is a proactive plan that is included in the IEP for students who qualify for special education services under IDEA.

PDD: Pervasive Developmental Disorder was first used in the 1980s to describe a class of disorders that commonly include impairments in social interaction, in imaginative activity, in verbal and nonverbal communication skills, and a limited number of interests and activities that tend to be repetitive. The DSM-IV identifies five disorders under the category of Pervasive Developmental Disorders: (1) Autistic Disorder, (2) Rett's Disorder, (3) Childhood Disintegrative Disorder, (4) Asperger's Disorder, and (5) Pervasive Developmental Disorder–Not Otherwise Specified, or PDD-NOS. Parents may note symptoms of PDD as early as infancy, and typically onset is prior to three years of age. PDD itself generally does not affect life expectancy. Occasionally some people use the term PDD as a general diagnostic label or as a short way of saying PDD-NOS. Still others may use the general category label of PDD because they are hesitant to diagnose very young children with a specific type of PDD, such as autism. Both approaches contribute to confusion about the term, because the term PDD actually refers to a category of disorders and is not a diagnostic label.

PDD-NOS: Pervasive Developmental Disorder–Not Otherwise Specified is a disorder listed in the DSM-IV under the class of Pervasive Developmental Disorders. To be diagnosed with PDD-NOS, an individual either does not fully meet the criteria of symptoms clinicians use to diagnose any of the four specific types of PDD, and/or the individual does not have the *degree* of impairment described in any of the above four PDD specific types. According to the DSM-IV, this category should be used "when there is a severe and pervasive impairment in the development of social interaction or verbal and nonverbal communication skills, or when stereotyped behavior, interests, and activities are present, but the criteria are not met for a specific Pervasive Developmental Disorder, Schizophrenia, Schizotypal Personality Disorder, or Avoidant Personality Disorder."[1]

PECS: Picture Exchange Communication System is a procedure for teaching functional communication that was developed in 1985 by Andy Bondy and Laurie Frost. PECS begins with teaching a student to exchange a picture of a desired item with a "teacher," who immediately honors the request. The training protocol is based on behavior analysis principles using prompting and reinforcement strategies that will lead to independent communication. Verbal prompts are not used, thus building immediate initiation and avoiding prompt dependency. The system goes on to teach discrimination of symbols and then how to put them all together in simple sentences. In the most advanced phases, individuals are taught to comment and to answer direct questions. Many preschoolers with ASD who have used PECS are reported to have developed speech.

Play Date is an arranged appointment for children to get together for a few hours to play and socialize. This is a preplanned interaction that provides an opportunity for children with ASD to learn new play and social skills through peer-directed interventions or to practice learned skills with new friends or in new environments.

R-4: Private Homeschool Affidavit is available in California. The R-4 Affidavit allows families to legally homeschool their children by establishing a private school in their home and complying with the private school requirements of the California Education Code. Parents who have established a home-based private school cannot be prosecuted for truancy. Exemptions under this section are valid only after verification by the attendance supervisor of the district that the private school has complied with the provisions of Education Code Section 33190, requiring the annual filing by the "owner or other head of a private school" of an affidavit of prescribed information with the Superintendent of Public Instruction. This affidavit does not act as a license. The Department of Education does not license, evaluate, recognize, approve, or endorse any private school course. The affidavit is necessary to effect public exemption from other schools and for the school to be eligible to receive the appropriate pupil records from the pupil's last school of attendance. This information is cited from the following Web site:

http://homeschooling.gomilpitas.com/regional/CaliforniaR4.htm

Replacement Behavior is the skill or skills that are taught to serve the same purpose or function as the inappropriate behavior that the parent wishes to eliminate. The replacement behavior is typically a communication or self-advocacy skill that allows the child to get his or her needs met in a more functional and prosocial way.

Rett's Disorder is also known as Rett Syndrome and is diagnosed primarily in females. In children with Rett's Disorder, development proceeds in an apparently normal fashion over the first six to eighteen months, at which point the parents notice a change in their child's behavior and some regression or loss of abilities, especially in gross motor skills such as walking and moving. This is followed by an obvious loss in abilities such as speech, reasoning, and hand use. The repetition of certain meaningless gestures or movements is an important clue to diagnosing Rett's Disorder; these gestures typically consist of constant hand-wringing or hand washing.[2]

RSP: Resource Specialist Program typically provides instructional support services to students with mild to moderate disabilities who are having difficulty with the general education curriculum in the areas of reading, writing, and mathematics. Students who receive RSP services usually require special education services for less than half of their school day and are assigned to general classroom teachers for the majority of the school day. Students receive resource specialist services as determined by the IEP team. The two typical service-delivery models are the "push in" model that provides services in the general education classroom or a "pull out" model where services are provided in a separate classroom either individually or in small groups.

RST: Resource Specialist Teacher is a teacher credentialed in Special Education who provides or heads a Resource Program. This specialized credential helps the teacher address a wide variety of learning disabilities. The RST is also skilled in assessment for learning disabilities, which may constitute a portion of their work, as well as in assessment of students meeting predefined goals. Some states may require a specific RST credential or certificate for a teacher placed in a Resource Program.

SDC: Special Day Class is an intensive educational program designed for students who have been found eligible for special education services. A qualifying student may receive special education services in an SDC if it is determined by the IEP team that this is the most appropriate environment in which to meet the educational goals. The range of intelligence level of children in a special day class measured by IQ can vary from below average to exceedingly high. As such, their academic instruction is usually adapted by an Independent Educational Plan (IEP) to fit each child's individual needs and capabilities. A special day class normally consists of a very small number of students. There is no set number of students that are assigned to an SDC, but some school districts do assign a class size. The classroom provides structure, accommodations, modification, and a setting that is available for the entire day or part of the day as outlined in the IEP. The special day class is staffed with at least one credentialed special education teacher and usually at least one assistant who help to provide the children with individualized instruction.

Self-Advocacy refers to people with disabilities taking control of their own lives, including being in charge of their own care in the educational or medical system. It means that although a person with a disability may call upon the support of others, the individual is entitled to be in control of their own resources and how they are directed. It includes knowing their rights and possessing the skills to make life decisions without undue influence or control by others. An example of self-advocacy is asking others for help with tasks with which the individual struggles. For individuals with ASD this may be organizational skills, self-help skills, or vocational skills.

Self-Awareness is the understanding of one's strengths, needs, disability, and rights. This is often a skill set that must be taught to individuals with ASD. Self-awareness is a critical building block for self-advocacy and self-determination.

Self-Determination is defined as the free choice of one's own acts without external controls. This involves developing an understanding of one's values and goals, as well as the self-advocacy skills to achieve the goals and outcomes the individual determines as important to him or her.

Self-Stimulating Behaviors refers to repetitive body movements or the repetitive movement of objects. This behavior is common in many individuals with developmental disabilities; however, it appears to be more common in autism. In fact, if a person with another developmental disability exhibits a form of self-stimulatory behavior, often the person is also labeled as having autistic characteristics. "Self-stim" or "stimming" can involve any one or all senses.

SIB: Self-Injurious Behavior is behavior that is inflicted by a person upon their own body without suicidal intent. These acts may be aimed at relieving otherwise unbearable emotions, sensations, or numbness. This is a behavior often seen in individuals with ASD who lack functional communication and who have more severe cognitive impairments. SIB can include hitting, biting, slapping, scratching, or pinching oneself. In more extreme cases, the individual can cause permanent tissue damage. This serious pattern of behavior should be given immediate attention to prevent escalation and to assess for possible underlying causes.

SLP: Speech and Language Pathologist is a credentialed professional who is trained to work with individuals who have a deficit in speech and language. They are sometimes called *speech therapists*. The SLP will assess, diagnose, treat, and help to prevent disorders related to speech, language, cognitive-communication, voice, swallowing, and fluency. Speech-language pathologists work with a variety of individuals who cannot produce speech sounds or cannot produce them clearly: those with speech rhythm and fluency problems, such as stuttering; people with voice disorders, such as inappropriate pitch or harsh voice; those with problems understanding and producing language; those who wish to improve their communication skills by modifying an accent; and those with cognitive communication impairments, such as attention, memory, and problem-solving disorders. They also work with people who have swallowing difficulties. SLP can play a major role in a program for a student with ASD because communication is one of the core deficit areas. The need for SLP services are assessed and included in the IEP for a student who qualifies for the services.

Stereotyped Behaviors are repetitive or ritualistic movements, postures, or utterances found in patients with cognitive delays, Autism Spectrum Disorders, tardive dyskinesia, and stereotypic movement disorder. Often called "stereotypies," these behaviors may involve simple movements such as body rocking, or complex movements, such as self-caressing, crossing and uncrossing of legs, and marching in place.

Stimming is a jargon term for a particular form of stereotypy, a repetitive body movement (often done unconsciously) that self-stimulates one or more senses in a regulated manner. It is shorthand for *self-stimulation,* and a stereotypy is referred to as *stimming* under the hypothesis that it has a function related to sensory input. Stereotypy is one of the symptoms listed by the DSM-IV for autism and is observed in about 10 percent of nonautistic young children. Many people with autism do not exhibit stereotypy. Common forms of stereotypy among people with autism include hand flapping, body spinning or rocking, lining up or spinning toys or other objects, echolalia, perseveration, and repeating rote phrases.

Support Network is a community of people who provide information, emotional support, resources, or services to assist the family or individual with special needs in the endeavors of life. Such networks can be formal or informal and can communicate face to face or through other means (for example, online, phone, telecommunications, and so on).

Thinking Tools are specific graphic organizers from the *Learning the R.O.P.E.S. for Improved Executive Functioning* curriculum by Patricia Schetter.[3] These tools are used to teach organizational skills and thinking to individuals on the autism spectrum or with other learning or behavioral disabilities.

ToM: Theory of Mind is the ability to attribute mental states—beliefs, intents, desires, pretending, knowledge, and so forth—to oneself and others and to understand that others have beliefs, desires, and intentions that are different from one's own. ToM is often significantly impaired or delayed in an individual on the autism spectrum and influences both academic and social competence. High cognitive abilities (IQ) have not been shown to correlate with ToM in these individuals.

Transition means a systematic plan for moving from one activity, setting, or situation to another. Educational transition planning takes place at the preschool level, when moving from grade to grade, and at age sixteen as indicated in IDEA in preparation for the transition from school to adult activities.

504 Plan refers to Section 504 of the Rehabilitation Act and the Americans with Disabilities Act, which specifies that no one with a disability can be excluded from participating in federally funded programs or activities, including elementary, secondary, or postsecondary schooling. "Disability" in this context refers to a "physical or mental impairment which substantially limits one or more major life activities." This can include physical impairments; illnesses or injuries; communicable diseases; chronic conditions such as asthma, allergies, and diabetes; and learning problems. A 504 plan spells out the modifications and accommodations that will be needed for these students to have an opportunity to perform at the same level as their peers, and might include such things as wheelchair ramps, blood-sugar monitoring, an extra set of textbooks, a peanut-free lunch environment, home instruction, or a tape recorder or keyboard for taking notes. Only certain classifications of disability are eligible for an IEP, and students who do not meet those classifications but still require some assistance to be able to participate fully in school could be candidates for a 504 plan. This could apply to some individuals who have AS or HFA and are performing well academically but struggle in other areas of functioning.

NOTES

Introduction

1. Centers for Disease Control (CDC). 1997. *CDC Releases New Data on Autism Spectrum Disorders from Multiple Communities in the United States.* Press Release. Atlanta, GA: CDC Online News Room, www.cdc.gov/media/index.html, February 2007.

Chapter One

1. Ozonoff, S., Rogers, S., and Hendron, D. O. *Autism Spectrum Disorders: A Research Review for Practitioners.* Arlington, VA: American Psychiatric Publishing, 2003, p. 22.

2. Ayres, A. J. *Sensory Integration and the Child.* Los Angeles: Western Psychological Services, 1979; Baranek, G. T., and Berkson, G. "Tactile Defensiveness in Children with Developmental Disabilities: Responsiveness and Habituation." *Journal of Autism and Developmental Disorders,* 1994, *24,* 457–471.

3. Dunn, W., Myles, B. S., and Orr, S. "Sensory Processing Associated with Asperger Syndrome: A Preliminary Investigation." *American Journal of Occupational Therapy,* 2002, 56(1),

97–102; Grandin, T. *Thinking in Pictures: And Other Reports from My Life with Autism.* New York: Doubleday, 1995.

4. Ozonoff, S., Rogers, S., and Hendron, D. O. *Autism Spectrum Disorders: A Research Review for Practitioners.* Arlington, VA: American Psychiatric Publishing, 2003.

5. Richdale, A. L., and Prior, M. R. "Urinary Cortisol Circadian Rhythm in a Group of High-Functioning Children with Autism." *Journal of Autism and Developmental Disorders,* 1992, *22*(3), 433–447.

6. Corbett, B., Mendoza, S., Abdullah, M., Wegelind, J., and Levine, S. "Cortisol Circadian Rhythms and Response to Stress in Children with Autism." *Psychoneuroendocrinology,* 2006, *31,* 59–68.

7. National Research Council. *Educating Children with Autism.* Washington, DC: National Academy Press, 2001.

8. Rogers, S. "Empirically Supported Comprehensive Treatments for Young Children with Autism." *Journal of Clinical Child Psychology,* 1998, *27,* 168–179.

9. Lovaas, O. I. "Behavioral Treatment and Normal Educational and Intellectual Functioning in Young Autistic Children." *Journal of Consulting and Clinical Psychology,* 1987, *55,* 3–9.

10. Baker, B. *Parent Training and Developmental Disabilities.* Washington, DC: American Association of Mental Retardation, 1989; Harris, S. L. *Families of the Developmentally Disabled: A Guide to Behavioral Intervention.* Elmsford, NY: Pergamon Press, 1983.

11. Sallows, G. O., and Graupner, T. D. "Intensive Behavioral Treatment for Children with Autism: Four-Year Outcome and Predictors." *American Journal on Mental Retardation,* 2005, *110*(6), 417–438.

12. Bristol. M. M., Galleghaer, J. J., and Holt, K. D. "Maternal Depressive Symptoms in Autism: Response to Psychoeducational Intervention." *Rehabilitation Psychology,* 1993, *38,* 3–9.

13. Koegel, R. L., and Koegel, L. K. *Teaching Children with Autism: Strategies for Initiating Positive Interactions and Improving Learning Opportunities.* Baltimore, MD: Paul H. Brookes, 1996.

14. Koegel, R. L., and others. "Collateral Effects of Parent Training on Families with Autistic Children." In R. F. Dangel & R. A. Polster (Eds.), *Parents Training: Foundations of Research and Practice.* New York: Guilford Press, 1984, pp. 358–378.

15. Rudner, L. M. "Scholastic Achievement and Demographic Characteristics of Home School Students in 1998." *Education Policy Analysis Archives,* 1999, *7*(8), 1–28.

16. Ray, B. D. *Strengths of Their Own: Home Schoolers Across America: Academic Achievement, Family Characteristics, and Longitudinal Traits.* Salem, OR: National Home Education Research Institute, 1997. (As reported in Medlin, 2000.)

17. Chatham-Carpenter, A. "Home Versus Public Schoolers: Differing Social Opportunities." *Home School Researcher,* 1994, *10*(1), 15–24; Medlin, R. G. "Home Schooling and the Question of Socialization." *Peabody Journal of Education,* 2000, *75*(1 & 2), 107–123.

18. Duvall, S. F., Ward, D. L., Delquadri, J. C., and Greenwood, C. R. "An Exploratory Study of Home School Instructional Environments and Their Effects of Basic Skill of Students with Learning Disabilities." *Education and Treatment of Children,* 1997, *20*(2), 150–172; Duvall, S. F., Delquadri, J. C., and Ward, D. L. "A Preliminary Investigation of the Effectiveness of Homeschool Instructional Environments for Students with Attention Deficit/Hyperactivity Disorder." *School Psychology Review,* 2004, *33*(1), 140–158.

19. Princiotta, D., and Bielick, S. *Homeschooling in the United States: 2003 Statistical Analysis Report* (NCES 2006–042). Washington, DC: U.S. Department of Education National Center for Educational Statistics, 2006.

20. McLeskey, J., Tyler, N. C., and Saunders Flippin, S. "The Supply of and Demand for Special Education Teachers: A Review of Research Regarding the Chronic Shortage of Special Education Teachers." *Journal of Special Education,* 2004, *38*(1), 5–21.

21. National Research Council. *Educating Children with Autism.* Washington, DC: National Academy Press, 2001, pp. 183–192; California Legislative Blue Ribbon Commission on Autism. *An Opportunity to Achieve Real Change for Californians with Autism Spectrum Disorders.* Sacramento: Legislative Office Building, 2007, pp. 45–52.

Chapter Two

1. Grandin, T. *Thinking in Pictures: And Other Reports from My Life with Autism.* New York: Doubleday, 1995; Hodgdon, L. *Visual Strategies for Improving Communication, Volume 1.* Troy, MI: Quirk Roberts Publishing, 1996; Cohen, M., and Sloan, D. *Visual Supports for People with Autism: A Guide for Parents and Professionals.* Bethesda, MD: Woodbine House, 2007; Savner, J., and Smith Myles, B. *Making Visual Supports Work in the Home and Community: Strategies for Individuals with Autism and Asperger Syndrome.* Shawnee Mission, KA: Autism Asperger Publishing, 2000.

2. Lovaas, O. I. "Behavioral Treatment and Normal Educational and Intellectual Functioning in Young Autistic Children." *Journal of Consulting and Clinical Psychology,* 1987, *55,* 3–9; Eikeseth, S., Smith, T., and Eldevik, E.J.S. "Intensive Behavioral Treatment at School for 4- to 7-Year-Old Children with Autism."

Behavior Modification, 2002, *26,* 49–68; National Research Council. *Educating Children with Autism.* Washington, DC: National Academy Press, 2001, p. 6.

3. National Research Council, *Educating Children with Autism.* Washington, DC: National Academy Press, 2001, p. 125.

4. Attwood, T. *Asperger's Syndrome: A Guide for Parents and Professionals.* London, UK, and Philadelphia, PA: Jessica Kingsley, 1998.

5. Holland, O. *Teaching at Home: A New Approach to Tutoring Children with Autism and Asperger Syndrome.* London, UK, and Philadelphia, PA: Jessica Kingsley, 2005.

Chapter Three

1. Dowty, T., and Cowlishaw, K. *Home Educating Our Autistic Spectrum Children: Paths Are Made by Walking.* London: Jessica Kingsley Publishers, 2002, p. 13.

2. Davis, M. *So—Why Do You Homeschool? Answering Questions People Ask About Home Education.* Longwood, FL: Xulon Press, 2005.

3. HomeSchool Association of California. *Empowering Families: Starting the Homeschool Journey.* Corona, CA: HSC, 2000–2005.

4. HomeSchool Association of California. *Empowering Families: Starting the Homeschool Journey.* Corona, CA: HSC, 2000–2005.

Chapter Four

1. Baldi, H., and Detmers, D. *Embracing Play* (DVD/Video). San Francisco: Behavioral Intervention Association, 2000. (Distributed by Woodbine House Special Needs Collection.)

2. Wolfberg, P. *Peer Play and the Autism Spectrum: The Art of Guiding Children's Socialization and Imagination.* Shawnee Mission, KA: Autism Asperger Publishing Company, 2000.

3. Baldi, H., and Detmers, D. *Passport to Friendship: Facilitating Peer Play for Children with ASD* (DVD/Video). San Francisco: Behavioral Intervention Association, 2006. (Distributed by Woodbine House Special Needs Collection.)

4. Howlin, P., Baron-Cohen, S., and Hadwin, J. *Teaching Children with Autism to Mind-Read.* West Sussex, England: John Wiley, 1999; McAfee, J. *Navigating the Social World: A Curriculum for Individuals with Asperger's Syndrome and High Functioning Autism.* Arlington, TX: Future Horizons, 2003.

5. Gray, C. *Comic Strip Conversations.* Arlington TX: Future Horizons, 1994. www.FutureHorizons-autism.com

6. Lighthall, K., and Schetter, P. *White Boards Words and Thoughts.* Redding, CA: Autism and Behavior Training Associates Publications and Products, 2008.

7. Gray, C. *Social Stories 10.0,* Jenison, MI: Jenison Public Schools, 2002, pp. 2–3.

8. Garcia-Winner, M. *Inside Out: What Makes a Person with Social Cognitive Deficits Tick?* San Jose, CA: Think Social Publishing, 2000. www.socialthinking.com

9. Linsenbach, S. *The Everything Homeschooling Book.* Avon, MA: Adams Media, an F + M Publication Company, 2003, p. 85.

10. Davies, A. *Teaching Asperger's Students Social Skills Through Acting: All Their World's a Stage!* Arlington, TX: Future Horizons, 2004. www.FutureHorizon-autism.com

11. Grandin, T., *The Unwritten Rules of Social Relationships.* Arlington, TX: Future Horizons, 2005, pp. 30–31.

12. Ozonoff, S., and Schetter, P. "Executive Dysfunction in Autism Spectrum Disorders: From Research to Practice." In

L. Metzler (ed.), *Executive Function in Education: From Theory to Practice.* New York: Guilford Publications, 2007.

13. Metzler, L. *Executive Function in Education: From Theory to Practice.* New York: The Guilford Press, 2007.

14. Schetter, P. *Learning the R.O.P.E.S. for Improved Executive Function.* Redding, CA: Autism and Behavior Training Associates, 2003. www.autismandbehavior.com

15. Rogers, S. "Empirically Supported Comprehensive Treatments for Young Children with Autism." *Journal of Clinical Child Psychology,* 1998, *27,* 168–179.

16. Grandin, T. 2005. *The Unwritten Rules of Social Relationships.* Arlington, TX: Future Horizons, 2005, pp. 30–31.

17. Kluth, P., and Schwarz, P. *Just Give Him the Whale! 20 Ways to Use Fascinations, Areas of Expertise, and Strengths to Support Students with Autism.* Baltimore, MD: Paul H. Brookes, 2008.

18. Gagnon, E. *Power Cards: Using Special Interests to Motivate Children and Youth with Asperger Syndrome and Autism.* Shawnee Mission, KA: Autism Asperger Publishing, 2001, p. 19.

19. Kranowitz, C. *The Out-of-Sync Child Has Fun: Activities for Kids with Sensory Integration Dysfunction.* New York: Perigee, 2003; Smith Myles, B., Tapscott-Cook, K., Miller, N., Rinner, L., and Robbins, L. *Asperger's Syndrome and Sensory Issues: Practical Solutions for Making Sense of the World.* Shawnee Mission, KA: Autism Asperger Publishing, 2001; Koomar, J., Kranowitz, C., Szklut, S., and others. *Answers to Questions Teachers Ask About Sensory Integration.* (3rd ed.) Arlington, TX: Future Horizons, 2007.

20. Frost, L., and Bondy, A. *PECS: The Picture Exchange Communication System.* Newark, DL: Pyramid Educational Products, 2002.

Chapter Five

1. Lighthall, K. *R.E.A.D.Y. for Inclusion: A Step-by-Step Process for Assessing and Implementing Successful Inclusive Education for Students with Autism Spectrum Disorders.* Redding, CA: ABTA Publications, 2007, 2008.

2. Lighthall, K. *What Makes School Great? Friends! Activities to Build Autism Awareness and Develop Friendship.* Redding, CA: ABTA Publications, 2008.

3. Linsenbach, S. *The Everything Homeschooling Book.* Avon, MA: Adams Media, an F + M Publication Company, 2003.

4. Cohen, C. Homeschooling: *The Teen Years: Your Complete Guide to Successfully Homeschooling the 13- to 18-Year-Old.* Roseville, CA: Prima Publishing, 2000.

5. Perner, L. E. "It's Not Too Early to Start Planning for College." *Autism-Asperger's Digest,* May–June 2003, pp. 33, 39.

6. Shore, S. *Beyond the Wall: Personal Experiences with Autism and Asperger Syndrome.* Shawnee Mission, KS: Autism Asperger Publishing Company, 2003.

7. Willey, L. *Pretending to Be Normal: Living with Asperger's Syndrome.* London, UK: Jessica Kingsley, 1999, p. 131.

8. Faherty, C., and Mesibov, G. *What Does It Mean to Me? A Workbook Explaining Self Awareness and Life Lessons to the Child or Youth with High-Functioning Autism or Asperger's.* Arlington, TX: Future Horizons Publishing, 2000; Gerland, G. *Finding Out About Asperger Syndrome, High Functioning Autism and PDD.* London, UK: Jessica Kingsley Publishers, 1997, 2000; Jackson, L. *Freaks, Geeks & Asperger Syndrome: A User Guide to Adolescence.* London, UK: Jessica Kingsley Publishers, 2002; Schnurr, R. *Asperger's Huh? A Child's Perspective.* Ontario,

Canada: Anisor Publishing, 1999; Yoshida, Y. *How to Be Yourself in a World That is Different: An Asperger Syndrome Study Guide for Adolescents.* London, UK: Jessica Kingsley Publishers, 2007.

9. Korin, E. S. *Asperger Syndrome: An Owner's Manual for Older Adolescents and Adults: What You, Your Parents and Friends, and Your Employer, Need to Know.* Shawnee Mission, KS: Autism Asperger Publishing, 2007; Shore, S. (ed.). *Ask and Tell: Self-Advocacy and Disclosure for People on the Autism Spectrum.* Shawnee Mission, KS: Autism Asperger Publishing, 2004.

10. Willey, L. *Pretending to Be Normal.* London, UK: Jessica Kingsley Publishers, 1999.

11. Sicile-Kira, C. *Adolescents on the Autism Spectrum: A Parent's Guide to the Cognitive, Social, Physical and Transition Needs of Teenagers with Autism Spectrum Disorders.* New York: Penguin Group, 2006.

12. Grandin, T., and Duffy, K. *Developing Talents: Careers for Individuals with Asperger Syndrome and High-Functioning Autism.* Shawnee Mission, KS: Autism Asperger Publishing, 2004.

13. Grandin, T., and Duffy, K. *Developing Talents: Careers for Individuals with Asperger Syndrome and High-Functioning Autism.* Shawnee Mission, KS: Autism Asperger Publishing, 2004; Grandin, T. *Thinking in Pictures: And Other Reports from My Life with Autism.* New York: Doubleday, 1995.

14. Perner, L. E. "Marketing a Person on the Autistic Spectrum: Some Business Lessons." *Soaring to New Heights: Proceedings of the Meeting of the Autism Society of America,* Seattle, 2004, pp. 246–253; Griffin, C., and Hammis, D. *Making Self-Employment Work for People with Disabilities.* Baltimore, MD: Brookes Publishing, 2003; Smith, M., Belcher, R., and Juhrs, P.

A Guide to Successful Employment for Individuals with Autism. Baltimore MD: Paul H. Brooks Publishing, 1995.

Chapter Six

1. Steinfeld, M. D., Weissmann, L., and Ajay, C. *Autism Spectrum Disorder (ASD): So You Have a Diagnosis, Now What?* November 2005. http://www.sacramentoasis.com/docs/8-22-03/mind_list.pdf.

Glossary of Terms and Acronyms

1. American Psychiatric Association. *Diagnostic and Statistical Manual of Mental Disorders, Fourth Edition (DSM-IV).* Washington, DC: American Psychiatric Association, 2004, pp. 77–78.

2. Moeschler, J., Gibbs, E., and Graham, J. Jr. *A Summary of Medical and Psychoeducation Aspects of Rett Syndrome.* Lebanon, NH: Clinical Genetics and Child Development Center, 1990.

3. Schetter, P. *Learning the R.O.P.E.S. for Improved Executive Functioning.* Woodland, CA: Autism and Behavior Training Associates, 2003.

INDEX

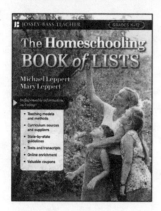

The Homeschooling Book of Lists

Michael Leppert and Mary Leppert

ISBN: 978-0-7879-9671-0
Paperback

"One of the most convenient and useful references I've seen—this book will be a blessing to countless parents, saving them time and helping them find just what they need, whatever their goals may be." —Andrew Pudewa, director, Institute for Excellence in Writing and homeschooling father

The Homeschooling Book of Lists is a comprehensive, authoritative, and user-friendly resource for homeschoolers or anyone considering teaching their child at home. Written by Michael and Mary Leppert, two experts in the field of homeschooling, this easy-to-use book is filled with information, tips, and resources that will help you give your child an outstanding education.

The book covers a wide variety of topics—including what to consider before homeschooling, state-by-state guidelines for homeschoolers, curriculum resources by subject area, and getting your homeschooled student into college. **The Homeschooling Book of Lists** offers:

- A variety of proven homeschooling models and methods
- Religious and ethnic homeschooling resources
- Guidance on finding help for special needs learners
- Information on tutors and tutoring, homeschooling suppliers, charter schools, and independent study programs
- Resources for testing and test preparation
- Valuable coupons to help you save money

In addition, this important resource contains frequently asked questions and a glossary of common homeschooling terms.

Other Books of Interest

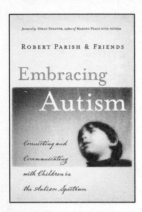

Embracing Autism

Connecting and Communicating with Children in the Autism Spectrum

Robert Parish

ISBN: 978-0-7879-9586-7
Hardcover

"While much has been written about the disability that is autism, little has been written about the people who live 'in the spectrum.' With this wonderful book Robert Parish has, with grace, humor, and hope, taken us beyond the diagnosis and into the real lives of individuals with autism and their families. Highly recommended for parents and professionals alike." —Peter F. Gerhardt, Ed.D., president and chair, Scientific Council, Organization for Autism Research, Baltimore, Maryland

Embracing Autism presents sensitive, sometimes humorous, experience-based stories from teachers, clinicians, and parent activists within the autism community. With insight and heart, this book offers parents and educators a way to better understand the world inhabited by ASD children and adults. Each story is compelling, inspirational, and informational—providing a vital and helpful perspective for anyone who is working or living day-to-day with ASD.

Embracing Autism gives readers encouragement for navigating the uncharted territory of working with an ASD child. Filled with passion and hope, *Embracing Autism* shows what makes people with ASD tick and gives useful information on how they communicate, learn, and ultimately what it takes to help them succeed.

ROBERT PARISH is an award-winning journalist with four nationally broadcast public TV documentaries about autism spectrum disorders to his credit. He has produced more than one hundred digital video projects about ASD for educational distribution and hosts a bimonthly program on Autism One Radio (www.autismone.org). Parish's son Jack has been an inspiration to him, his family, and many others. Thousands visit his educational website each month at www.comebackjack.org.

Other Books of Interest

Social Skills Activities for
Special Children

Darlene Mannix

ISBN: 978-0-470-25935-1
Paperback

Over 160 ready-to-use lessons and worksheets to help children use social skills inside and outside the classroom

"Offers elementary teachers a comprehensive social-emotional skills curriculum . . . This book belongs on every teacher's bookshelf!"
—Nick Elksnin, Ph.D., NCSP, Learning and Evaluation Resources and Linda K. Elksnin, Ph.D., professor emerita, The Citadel; authors of *Teaching Social-Emotional Skills at School and Home*

"A terrific resource...The comprehensive selection of topics addresses real, complex social interactions encountered in schools and communities today."
—Chris Schnieders, Ph.D., director of teacher training, Frostig Center

This thoroughly revised and updated second edition of the groundbreaking *Social Skills Activities for Special Children* offers teachers 164 ready-to-use lessons—complete with reproducible worksheets—that help children become aware of acceptable social behavior and acquire basic social skills.

Each of the book's lessons highlights a specific skill framed in real-life situations. This gives teachers a meaningful way to guide students to think about why a particular social skill is important. The practical hands-on activities that accompany each lesson help students work through, think about, discuss, and practice the skill in or outside of the classroom.

Other Books of Interest

Social Skills Activities for
Secondary Students with Special
Needs

Darlene Mannix

ISBN: 978-0-4702-5936-8
Paperback

**A flexible, ready-to-use activities program to help
special students in grades 6-12**

"Darlene Mannix's Social Skills for Secondary Students with Special
Needs *does what many books don't do—it promotes use of social-
emotional skills with peers and adults across a variety of settings.
Teachers will find this book practical and easy to use."*

—Nick Elksnin, Ph.D., NCSP, Learning and Evaluation Resources and
Linda K. Elksnin, Ph.D., professor emerita, The Citadel; authors of
Teaching Social-Emotional Skills at School and Home

The updated new edition of this valuable resource offers an exciting
collection of 200 ready-to-use worksheets to help adolescents build the
social skills they need to interact effectively with others and learn how to
apply these skills to various real-life settings, situations, and problems.
The book provides 20 complete teaching units focusing on 20 basic social
skills, such as being a good listener, "reading" other people, and using
common sense.

DARLENE MANNIX, MA, has 26 years of experience as a classroom
teacher and is the bestselling author of numerous books for special
educators, including *Social Skills Activities for Special Children* (978-0-
87628-868-9), *Life Skills Activities for Special* Children (978-0-87628-
547-3), *Writing Skills Activities for Special Children* (978-0-7879-7884-
6), and *Character Building Activities for Kids* (978-0-13-042585-0).

Other Books of Interest

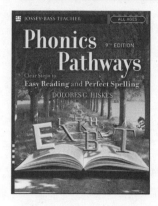

Phonics Pathways
Clear Steps to Easy Reading and Perfect Spelling
9th Edition

Dolores G. Hiskes

ISBN: 978-0-7879-7910-2
Paperback

"I had no idea how to teach phonics, yet in about six weeks my 3-1/2 and 5-year-old children were reading and spelling. I always recommend Phonics Pathways—*it remains my favorite program."*

> —Sandra S. Elam, director, The National Right to Read Foundation

Now in its ninth edition, *Phonics Pathways* (with help from Dewey the Bookworm) teaches students of all ages the rudiments of phonics and spelling with an efficient, practical, and foolproof method. Written in an easy-to-use format, *Phonics Pathways* is organized by sounds and spelling patterns. The patterns are introduced one at a time and slowly built into syllables, words, phrases, and sentences.

Printed in a large 8-1/2" x 11" lay-flat format for easy photocopying, *Phonics Pathways* is filled with illustrative examples, word lists, and practice readings that are 100 percent decodable. While appropriate for K-2 emergent readers, this award-winning book has also been used successfully with adolescent and adult learners, as well as second language learners and students with learning disabilities such as dyslexia. *Phonics Pathways* is ideal for school, tutoring, and home use.

DOLORES G. HISKES has tutored reading for over thirty years and trained teachers from all over the world. She has implemented a number of school and community tutoring programs, such as the highly touted YES Reading Center in Palo Alto, CA. Well-published in professional journals and a winner of numerous honors, she publishes a free on-line newsletter about teaching reading, called Phonics Talk (www.dorbooks.com).

Other Books of Interest

Differentiated Instruction Made Easy

Hundreds of Multi-Level Activities for All Learners

Phyllis Kaplan, Virginia Rogers, and Rande Webster

ISBN: 978-0-470-37235-7
Paperback

Differentiated Instruction Made Easy is a hands-on resource designed to aid teachers in supporting the individual learning needs of their students as they participate in similar tasks. Teachers will find hundreds of creative ideas that will motivate and reinforce learning for all students in grades 2-8. The book's dynamic activities are targeted to specific subject areas and will help students to experience success despite their learning challenges.

Differentiated Instruction Made Easy contains:

- Ready-to-use activities that support the teaching of standards-based subjects across the curriculum
- Tools for reading, math, science, and written expression
- Chapters on art, music, media, service learning, and peace
- Teacher-student contracts, multi-level game boards, spinners, task cards and wheels, and open-ended add-ons

Teachers can use the book to encourage students to design their own games, task wheels, and activities reflecting their individual interests and strengths. *Differentiated Instruction Made Easy* helps teachers tap into each child's passion—the first step to developing students who are truly motivated to learn.